SAMS
Teach
Yourself

MySQL®

Chris Newman

in **10**
Minutes

SAMS   800 East 96th Street, Indianapolis, Indiana, 46240 USA

Sams Teach Yourself MySQL® in 10 Minutes

Copyright © 2006 by Sams Publishing

International Standard Book Number: 0-672-32863-1

Library of Congress Catalog Card Number: 2005328631

Printed in the United States of America

Fourth Printing February 2010

14   13   12   11   10   9   8   7   6   5   4

Trademarks

Warning and Disclaimer

Bulk Sales

Sams Publishing offers excellent discounts on this book when ordered in quantity for bulk purchases or special sales. For more information, please contact

U.S. Corporate and Government Sales
1-800-382-3419
corpsales@pearsontechgroup.com

For sales outside of the U.S., please contact

International Sales
international@pearsoned.com

ACQUISITIONS EDITOR
Shelley Johnston

DEVELOPMENT EDITOR
Damon Jordan

MANAGING EDITOR
Charlotte Clapp

PROJECT EDITOR
Andy Beaster

COPY EDITOR
Krista Hansing

INDEXER
Juli Bess

PROOFREADER
Kathy Bidwell

TECHNICAL EDITOR
Adam DeFields

PUBLISHING COORDINATOR
Vanessa Evans

INTERIOR DESIGNER
Gary Adair

COVER DESIGNER
Aren Howell

PAGE LAYOUT
Nonie Ratcliff

Contents

PART 3   Advanced SQL

PART 6   Interfacing with MySQL

PART 7   Appendixes

About the Author

Chris Newman is a consultant programmer who specializes in database development with an Internet twist. He has extensive commercial experience in using PHP to integrate various database systems, and he has produced a wide range of applications for an international client base.

A graduate of Keele University, Chris lives in Stoke-on-Trent, England, where he runs Lightwood Consultancy, Ltd., the company he founded in 1999 to further his interest in online database development.

Chris has served as a technical editor on several books from Sams, including *PHP and MySQL Web Development* (2004), *Sams Teach Yourself PHP, MySQL, and Apache All in One* (2004), and *Red Hat Fedora Unleashed* (2004). He is the author of *Sams Teach Yourself PHP in 10 Minutes* (2005) and *SQLite* (2004), and co-author of *MySQL Phrasebook* (2006).

More information on Lightwood Consultancy, Ltd., is available at http://www.lightwood.net. Chris can be contacted at chris@lightwood.net.

Acknowledgments

I would like to thank the team at Sams Publishing for its ongoing support and guidance while writing this book. Special thanks to Shelley Johnston, who hired me as a technical editor and then one day asked if I wanted to write. Indeed I did! After six awesome years working together, Shelley is moving on, and I wish her every happiness.

We Want to Hear from You!

As the reader of this book, *you* are our most important critic and commentator. We value your opinion and want to know what we're doing right, what we could do better, what areas you'd like to see us publish in, and any other words of wisdom you're willing to pass our way.

You can email or write me directly to let me know what you did or didn't like about this book—as well as what we can do to make our books stronger.

Please note that I cannot help you with technical problems related to the topic of this book, and that due to the high volume of mail I receive, I might not be able to reply to every message.

When you write, please be sure to include this book's title and author as well as your name and phone or email address. I will carefully review your comments and share them with the author and editors who worked on the book.

Email: opensource@samspublishing.com

Mail: Mark Taber
           Associate Publisher
           Sams Publishing
           800 East 96th Street
           Indianapolis, IN 46240 USA

Reader Services

Visit our website and register this book at www.samspublishing.com/register for convenient access to any updates, downloads, or errata that might be available for this book.

Introduction

MySQL is a powerful relational database-management system that supports a richly featured SQL language. It's fast, easy to use, and—best of all—available for free!

MySQL is a very popular choice for web development because of its close relationship with PHP. Many companies provide MySQL as part of a standard web-hosting deal, so you might already have access to MySQL without needing to install any software.

Sams Teach Yourself MySQL in 10 Minutes is designed to help you get a handle on MySQL quickly and easily through a series of step-by-step lessons.

Who Is This Book For?

This book is for you if any (or all) of the following apply:

- You're new to MySQL.

- You want to quickly learn how to be productive with a MySQL database.

- You want to learn how to use MySQL for your own applications.

How This Book Works

Sams Teach Yourself MySQL in 10 Minutes is divided into 25 lessons that gradually build on one another. By the end of the book, you should have a solid understanding of MySQL and know how to use it in a variety of real-world situations.

Each lesson is written in simple steps so that you can quickly grasp the overall concept and put it into practice. The lessons are also designed to stand alone so that you can jump directly to particular topics as needed.

Online Support Files and Appendixes

The sample database used in *Sams Teach Yourself MySQL in 10 Minutes* can be downloaded from the Sams Publishing website, at http://www.samspublishing.com/. You can install this database on your own MySQL server to follow every example in the book. There are also four bonus appendixes that can be downloaded from the Sams Publishing website: Appendix C, "SQL Syntax Reference," Appendix D, "MySQL Datatype Reference," Appendix E, "Configuration Reference," and Appendix F, "MySQL Reserved Words."

Conventions Used in This Book

This book uses different typefaces to differentiate between SQL code and other content.

SQL code is presented using monospace type. Bold text indicates user input.

 A Note presents pertinent pieces of information related to the surrounding discussion.

 A Caution advises you about potential problems that involve MySQL or its implementation.

 A Tip offers advice or demonstrates an easier way to do something.

LESSON 1
Introducing MySQL

In this lesson, you learn what the MySQL database system is and what it can do.

Database Basics

At its very simplest, a database is an organized way of holding together various pieces of information. The term *database* actually refers to the collection of data, not the means by which it is stored. For a computer database, the software used to manage the data is known as a database-management system (DBMS).

A database need not be stored on computer—although, of course, that is what this book is about! A filing cabinet and a telephone directory both contain databases: They hold information, organized in a structured manner so that you can easily access the individual item you want to find.

Relational Databases

MySQL is a relational database-management system (RDBMS). The term *relational* indicates that MySQL can store its data as a number of different tables that are related to each other in some way.

The advantage of this type of database over a flat table system is that very large databases can be constructed from different tables, each of which contains only information relevant to that table.

Much has been written about relational database theory, but you need to understand only a little to create efficient databases. You don't need to be scared by what appears to be a very academic topic—a great deal of the principles of relational database design are grounded in common sense. You will learn more about this in Lesson 16, "Designing Your Database."

Why Use MySQL?

You can choose from many different RDBMS options, so why use MySQL over another system?

One of the primary factors when choosing an RDBMS is cost. MySQL is distributed as open-source software under the GNU General Public License, so you can actually use MySQL free of charge.

Also available for MySQL is a commercial license that includes various levels of technical support for users with mission-critical systems. Even with the cost of commercial support, MySQL offers a significantly lower total cost of ownership over other enterprise-level RDBMS.

MySQL is robust, powerful, and scalable. It can be used in applications from tiny web databases to very large data warehouses with terabytes of data. You can use MySQL replication or clustering to guarantee 100% availability. A number of case studies published on MySQL.com give an example of just what MySQL is capable of.

 Case Studies You can read about how MySQL has been used in large projects at http://www.mysql.com/why-mysql/case-studies/.

Anatomy of a Database

A database consists of a series of tables. Each table has a name, which is how it is referenced in the SQL language. Each database also has a name, and the same RDBMS can manage many different databases. MySQL is a multiuser database and can restrict access to each database to only specific users.

A database table looks somewhat like a spreadsheet: a set of rows and columns that can contain data at each intersection. In a relational database, you store different types of data in different tables. For instance, the sample database in this book has separate tables for customers, products, and orders.

Each table has a defined set of columns, which determine the values it can store. For example, the table that contains information about products needs to store a name, price, and weight for every product. Each row of data can contain values for only the columns defined in the table.

In addition, each column is defined as a particular data type, which determines the kind of values it can store. The data type might restrict values to numeric or date values, or it might impose a maximum size.

What Is SQL?

The Structured Query Language (SQL) is the most common way to retrieve and manage database information. An SQL query consists of a series of keywords that define the data set you want to fetch from the database. SQL uses descriptive English keywords, so most queries are easy to understand.

> **SQL** Sometimes you will hear *SQL* pronounced as the word *sequel,* but it's also okay to pronounce it as the letters *S-Q-L.*

Virtually every RDBMS on the market uses the SQL language. The MySQL implementation of SQL conforms to the ANSI SQL standards and implements some of its own extension to handle features that are specific to MySQL.

About MySQL AB and mysql.com

MySQL AB is the Swedish company that develops, maintains, and markets the MySQL database server and tools.

MySQL Source   Although MySQL is distributed as open-source software, MySQL AB owns the source code to MySQL and determines the terms under which it is made available. Currently, MySQL is distributed under the GNU General Public License.

MySQL AB provides technical support to users with commercial support packages. The company also runs MySQL training courses around the world and issues MySQL Certification to those who want to become accredited MySQL Developers or Database Administrators.

The MySQL website, http://www.mysql.com/, contains a section called Developer Zone (which you can access directly at http://dev.mysql.com/) where you can find online support in the form of forums, mailing lists, and user groups. Consider joining one of the online communities; they are a great way to learn more about MySQL from other users.

You can download or view online (in the Developer Zone) a comprehensive reference manual for MySQL. You can download a printable PDF version or browse an HTML-format manual that is fully searchable.

Online Manual   You can use the shortcut URL http://www.mysql.com/*ANYTHING* to search the online manual for *ANYTHING*. If there is an exact match, you will be taken straight to the appropriate page; otherwise, you will see a list of possible matches.

Other Resources

A number of MySQL books have been published under the MySQL Press brand. Currently, these include *MySQL Tutorial* (2004), *MySQL Language Reference* (2005), *MySQL Administrator's Guide* (2005), and *MySQL Certification Study Guide* (2004).

You can view the current range of MySQL Press titles at
http://dev.mysql.com/books/mysqlpress/index.html.

MySQL Components

Let's take a moment to look at where MySQL will reside on your system.
If you do not yet have MySQL installed, refer to Appendix A, "Installing
MySQL."

Linux/UNIX Systems

The location of MySQL programs, libraries, and other files depends on
the installation prefix used when MySQL was installed. Typically, the prefix is either /usr/mysql or /usr/local/mysql.

In the location used on your system, you will find the following subdirectories:

- bin—Contains the MySQL executables, including the database
  server and all the client programs

- lib—Contains the development libraries used to communicate
  with a MySQL database from your own programs

- include—Contains the header files required to use MySQL
  APIs

- data—The MySQL data directory, containing the actual database files

- support_files—A number of sample configuration files

The MySQL configuration file is named my.cnf. The file /etc/my.cnf
contains global settings, but you can also create a file named my.cnf in
the data directory that applies only to that MySQL server; it is possible to
have multiple MySQL servers on one machine.

RPMs If you used a packaged installation method such as RPM, the system programs might have been installed to common locations alongside other applications. In this case, the data directory is /var/lib/mysql.

Path Make sure that the MySQL bin directory is in your system path so you can avoid having to enter the full path to the client programs when you want to run them. Refer to your operating system documentation for details on how to set this up.

Windows Systems

The default install location is C:\Program Files\MySQL. The system is installed in a subfolder that is named using the MySQL minor version number. For example, MySQL 5.0.18 is installed to C:\Program Files\MySQL\MySQL Server 5.0.

In the version-specific install location, you will find the following subdirectories:

- bin—The MySQL server and client program executables

- data—The MySQL data directory, containing the actual database files

In the installation directory, you will also find a number of sample configuration files. The current configuration is found in my.ini located in this folder.

MySQL is installed as a Windows service. To start and stop the database server, go to Control Panel, Administrative Tools, and select Services. A program group in the Start menu contains a shortcut to the mysql monitor program and the configuration wizard.

Summary

In this lesson, you took your first step with MySQL. You learned a little about what MySQL can do and how to find support when things go wrong. In the next lesson, you'll learn how to connect to a MySQL database using the mysql program.

LESSON 2
Using MySQL

In this lesson, you learn how to connect to a MySQL database and use the mysql command-line program.

The mysql Client

The mysql program is a command-line client used for sending commands to a MySQL server. It can be used to enter SQL commands to query a database or alter table definitions; it also has its own set of commands to control its operation.

 The mysql Program   In this lesson and throughout this book, mysql—printed in lower case—refers specifically to the MySQL command-line client program.

Starting the Command-Line Client

To start the command-line client, simply invoke the `mysql` program from the command line. If your local MySQL server allows anonymous connections, you can invoke `mysql` without any additional switches. The result looks similar to the following:

```
$ mysql
Welcome to the MySQL monitor.  Commands end with ; or \g.
Your MySQL connection id is 2084 to server version:
➥4.1.12-standard-log

Type 'help;' or '\h' for help. Type '\c' to clear the buffer.

mysql>
```

The `mysql>` prompt indicates that you will now be typing commands into the mysql client instead of the system shell.

When MySQL is first installed, anonymous connections are allowed unless you disable them. It is a good idea to remove anonymous user access; this is discussed in Appendix A, "Installing MySQL."

If your server does not allow anonymous connections, you will see an error like the following when you attempt to start the mysql program:

```
$ mysql
ERROR 1045 (28000): Access denied for user 'chris'@'localhost'
(using password: NO)
```

If you will be using mysql to connect to a remote database and there is no local MySQL server, or if the local MySQL server is not running, the error will look like this:

```
$ mysql
ERROR 2002 (HY000): Can't connect to local MySQL server through
socket '/var/lib/mysql/mysql.sock' (2)
```

Connecting to MySQL

Even if your database does allow anonymous connections, you will need to connect using a username and password to do anything useful. To connect to a MySQL database, you must know the connection parameters to use.

Because MySQL can accept connections over a network, you must specify the database server hostname. If you are connecting to a MySQL server running on the local machine, the hostname is *localhost*. Otherwise, you can use the IP address or hostname of the remote server.

You also need to supply a username and password to authenticate with the database server. As you will learn in Lesson 18, "Managing User Access," the username and password to access a database can be locked down so that they work only when you connect from a specific location.

Finally, you must supply the database name to connect to. Each username may have access to one or more databases on the server; you must authenticate to gain access to your own databases.

The mysql program accepts a number of switches to specify how to connect to a database. Use the --user switch to supply a username, and use the --password switch to supply a password, as shown:

```
$ mysql --user=yourname --password=yourpass
```

Note that using this command as shown means that your password is visible onscreen. To avoid this, use the --password switch without an argument to be presented with a password entry prompt.

```
$ mysql --user=yourname --password
Enter password:
```

Enter your password when prompted to log on to the MySQL server. Note that your password is not displayed onscreen as you type.

Windows Menu On Windows systems, there is a menu item in the MySQL program group named MySQL Command Line Client. Selecting this item invokes mysql with a connection to the local server using the username root; you are prompted to enter a password to continue.

If there is a problem authenticating with the MySQL server using either of these methods, you will see an error like this:

```
ERROR 1045 (28000): Access denied for user
➥'yourname'@'localhost'
(using password: YES)
```

To connect to a database on a remote server, use the --host switch.

```
$ mysql --host=host.yourdomain.com --user=yourname --password
```

The value given in --host can be the IP address of the server or a fully qualified domain name.

Remote Connections   Remember that your firewall must be configured to allow you to access the MySQL port if you need to connect to a remote database.

Each of the connection parameter switches to `mysql` has a shorter version that you can use, if you prefer. The `--user` switch can be replaced by `-u`, and `--password` by `-p`. When using the shorter switches, note that the equals sign is not needed—the value is given immediately after the switch.

For instance, the following two commands are identical:

```
$ mysql --user=yourname --password
```

```
$ mysql -uyourname -p
```

The `--host` switch can be abbreviated to `-h` in the same way, as shown in the following command:

```
$ mysql -hhost.yourdomain.com -uyourname -p
```

MySQL Port   The default port for connections to MySQL over a network is 3306. If your server uses a different port number, specify it using `--port=` or `-P` when connecting using mysql.

The `--database` switch can be abbreviated to `-D`. In fact, the `--database` or `-D` switch can be omitted, and you can just specify the database at the end of the `mysql` command, as shown:

```
$ mysql -hhost.yourdomain.com -uyourname -ppassword dbname
```

Password Argument   When using the short connection switches, make sure that there is no space between –p and the password. Otherwise, you will be prompted to enter a password, and the password you gave on the command line will be treated as the database name.

Executing SQL Statements

Now let's look at how the mysql program is used to execute a SQL statement on a MySQL database.

Selecting a Database to Use

Your username and password give you access to one or more specific databases. For instance, if you are using a MySQL server provided by your web host, your username will give you access only to the database that is included with your web space. Other customers have their own individual passwords.

When you are connected to MySQL, issue the show databases command to see which databases are available to you. The SHOW DATABASES command is specific to MySQL but is executed through the mysql program like all other SQL commands.

```
mysql> SHOW DATABASES;
+-------------------+
| Database          |
+-------------------+
| mysql             |
| test              |
| yourdb            |
+-------------------+
3 rows in set (0.00 sec)
```

To select the database named yourdb, use the \u command along with the database name.

```
mysql> \u yourdb
Database changed
```

Built-In Commands   Commands that begin with a
backslash are internal commands for the mysql monitor program, not part of the SQL command set.

If you attempt to connect to a database that does not exist, or if you
mistype the name, you will see an error message.

```
mysql> \u wrongdb
ERROR 1049 (42000): Unknown database 'wrongdb'
```

You can also specify the database to connect to by using the --database
or –D switch to the mysql program.

```
$ mysql --user=yourname --database=yourdb --password
```

In fact, the mysql program enables you to put a database name after all
the switches have been given without prefixing it with --database or –D.
The following is, therefore, equivalent to the previous command:

```
$ mysql --user=yourname --password yourdb
```

Showing Connection Status

The \s command returns the status of the current database connection,
including the current database name and the connection parameters.

If you are using several databases at the same time, issuing \s is a handy
way to find out which one you are working on at any given time. The following output shows a connection to a MySQL 4.1 server running on a
local Windows machine:

```
mysql> \s
--------------
C:\Program Files\MySQL\MySQL Server 4.1\bin\mysql.exe
Ver 14.7 Distrib 4.1.14, for Win32 (ia32)
Connection id:          94
Current database:       mysqlin10
Current user:           root@localhost
SSL:                    Not in use
Using delimiter:        ;
Server version:         4.1.14-nt
```

```
Protocol version:        10
Connection:              localhost via TCP/IP
Server characterset:     latin1
Db      characterset:    latin1
Client characterset:     latin1
Conn. characterset:      latin1
TCP port:                3306
Uptime:                  35 days 5 hours 34 min 51 sec

Threads: 1  Questions: 542843  Slow queries: 18  Opens: 546
Flush tables: 1  Open tables: 0  Queries per second avg: 0.178
- - - - - - - - - - - - - -
```

 Reconnecting   To force a reconnect to the database server, issue the \r command.

Entering a SQL Command

Although you will not learn specific SQL commands until the next lesson, here you should understand how to execute SQL statements through mysql.

Because SQL commands can span many lines, you must use a semicolon to tell MySQL that a command is finished.

Look back to the SHOW DATABASES command, in the section "Selecting a Database to Use." You'll see that it required a semicolon at the end of the command. If this had been omitted, the text on your screen would look like this instead:

```
mysql> SHOW DATABASES
    ->
```

When you press the Enter key and a command has not been terminated, the prompt changes from mysql> to ->, indicating that you are continuing a command from the previous line of input. You can enter a semicolon at any time to terminate the statement, and your SQL command can span as many lines as necessary before being terminated.

Consider the following SQL query (you do not need to understand how it works yet), entered in mysql. The result of the query from the sample tables used in the book appears directly underneath the query.

```
mysql> SELECT first_name, last_name
    -> FROM customer_contacts
    -> WHERE customer_code = 'PRESINC'
    -> ORDER BY last_name;
+------------+-----------+
| first_name | last_name |
+------------+-----------+
| Abraham    | Lincoln   |
| Richard    | Nixon     |
| Franklin   | Roosevelt |
| Theodore   | Roosevelt |
+------------+-----------+
4 rows in set (0.00 sec)
```

The mysql program enables you to continue entering the query one line at a time; it sends the query to the MySQL server for execution only when you enter the semicolon to terminate the statement.

The query results are displayed in tabular format, just as you saw for SHOW DATABASES. The only difference this time is that there are two columns in the table. This format will quickly become familiar—it is the default output format for all SQL queries executed through mysql.

Underneath the query results is shown the total number of records retrieved by the query and the total execution time required to produce the results. In this example, the execution time appears to be zero—in fact, the time taken by the MySQL server was less than one hundredth of a second. Only when you begin to create complex queries will you notice a significant execution time.

When No Records Are Retrieved

If your query returns no rows, MySQL returns no data and no error message. The following example shows the response produced:

```
mysql> SELECT *
    -> FROM emptytable;
Empty set (0.00 sec)
```

Instead of the row count, mysql shows the message `Empty set`. The execution time is still displayed.

Query Output Formats

Instead of using a semicolon terminator symbol, the mysql client provides two built-in commands that send your query to the MySQL server. The \g command immediately executes the query being entered and displays the results onscreen.

However, if you use \G instead of \g, the query results are displayed in a vertical format instead of the usual tabular layout. This format produces one row of output for each column in the database, as shown:

```
mysql> SELECT * FROM products
    -> \G
*************************** 1. row ***************************
  code: MINI
  name: Small product
weight: 1.50
 price: 5.99
*************************** 2. row ***************************
  code: MIDI
  name: Medium product
weight: 4.50
 price: 9.99
*************************** 3. row ***************************
  code: MAXI
  name: Large product
weight: 8.00
 price: 15.99
3 rows in set (0.02 sec)
```

Vertical Format   The vertical query format is very useful when you want to view a single row of data from a table. The tabular layout might produce output that is too wide for your screen if the table contains many columns.

You can also change the default output format to vertical by starting mysql with the - -vertical switch. Then simply terminating a query with a semicolon will produce output in this format.

 Other Formats   Other format options that can be selected with switches when mysql is invoked are - -html and - -xml. These produce HTML table and XML data output, respectively.

Editing a SQL Command

MySQL provides the capability to easily edit the last SQL statement you entered so that you can make a small change or correction to your query without needing to retype it in full.

Use the \e command to open an editor containing the current query. The actual editor used depends on your system environment; this is usually vi or vim, unless you specify otherwise.

 Changing Editors   To change the query editor, set the name of the program you want to use in the EDITOR environment variable.

After you edit and save the query, you are returned to the mysql client with the prompt showing ->. It is as if you had just entered the query at the command line. To execute the query again, enter a semicolon or use the \g or \G commands.

Most modern systems also support command-line editing. You can use the left and right cursor keys to move along the line currently being entered to change text as you type. You can also use the up and down keys to cycle through the command history and retrieve commands that you entered earlier in the session.

Starting Over   If you want to start again with a new SQL statement without running the command being entered, issue the \c command to clear the current command and return to the mysql> prompt.

Capturing Output from MySQL

If you want to divert the output of a SQL query to a log file, use the \T command along with a filename. For instance, to write the output of a query to query.txt, do the following:

```
mysql> \T output.txt
Logging to file 'query.txt'
```

Any queries subsequently executed in mysql will be appended to query.txt and will be displayed onscreen. The retrieved data and the query itself are both written to the file—in fact, the log file records exactly what is displayed onscreen.

To stop writing to a log file, the \t command cancels any previously issued \T commands.

Exiting the mysql Program

To exit the mysql program, use the \q command. Alternatively, you can type quit or exit to leave the program.

If you want to run a single host command without exiting mysql, use the \! command. The following example runs the system command pwd on a UNIX/Linux system to determine the path of the current working directory:

```
mysql> \! pwd
/home/chris/public_html
```

Creating the Sample Tables

Before moving on to the next lesson, you need to create the sample database tables that are used in this book.

Installing the Sample Tables

You can download a SQL file that contains all the instructions needed to create the sample tables from www.samspublishing.com.

Save this file to your hard disk as `sampdb.sql` and issue the following command:

```
$ mysql --user=yourname --password dbname < sampdb.sql
```

The < symbol causes the contents of `sampdb.sql` to be passed to the mysql program all at once. The result is that the sample tables are created within the database you specified.

Summary

In this lesson, you learned how to connect to a MySQL database using the mysql program. In the next lesson, you will learn how to create a simple SQL query to retrieve data from MySQL.

LESSON 3
Retrieving Data

In this lesson, you learn how to use a SELECT statement to fetch records from a MySQL database.

The SELECT Statement

The first SQL command you will learn, and the one you will use most frequently, is SELECT. In this lesson, you begin by learning how to fetch data records from a single table.

A SELECT statement begins with the SELECT keyword and is used to retrieve information from MySQL database tables. You must specify the table name to fetch data from—using the FROM keyword—and one or more columns that you want to retrieve from that table.

 Keywords and Statements A *keyword* is a word that is part of the SQL language. In the examples in this book, SQL keywords are always written in capitals, although they are not case sensitive.

A SQL *statement* begins with a keyword and can contain several more keywords that must appear in the correct, structured way—known as the statement's *syntax*.

Retrieving Individual Columns

If you execute the following SQL statement using mysql, the output produced will be as shown:

```
mysql> SELECT name
    -> FROM customers;
+---------------------------+
| name                      |
+---------------------------+
| Presidents Incorporated   |
| Science Corporation       |
| Musicians of America      |
+---------------------------+
3 rows in set (0.02 sec)
```

 Terminating a Statement   Remember that the semi-colon character is required to indicate the end of a SQL statement. Alternatively, you can use the `go` command or `\g` to tell mysql to execute a query.

The customers table contains three records. In this statement, we tell MySQL to fetch the value of the name column; this is displayed for every record in the table.

The data displayed is not ordered. Usually records are retrieved in the same order in which they were inserted into the database. In this example, the company names are displayed in the order in which they were inserted in the sample table-creation script.

 Order of Records   Although records are normally retrieved in the order in which they are inserted into the database, you cannot rely on a particular order being preserved. If your database is backed up and restored, or if a maintenance operation is performed on the database, MySQL might alter the order in which records are stored internally.

A SELECT statement will return every row from the table unless you tell it otherwise. You will learn how to do this, by putting a filter on the query, in the next lesson.

Retrieving Multiple Columns

Now you'll try another simple SELECT statement, this time on the products table. You can retrieve the values from two columns in the same query by specifying a list of columns after the SELECT keyword, separating them with a comma.

```
mysql> SELECT name, price
    -> FROM products;
+----------------+-------+
| name           | price |
+----------------+-------+
| Small product  |  5.99 |
| Medium product |  9.99 |
| Large product  | 15.99 |
+----------------+-------+
3 rows in set (0.01 sec)
```

The columns in the output appear in the order given in the query. To add the weight column to the data retrieved, add it to the end of the list of columns selected, as follows:

```
mysql> SELECT name, price, weight
    -> FROM products;
+----------------+-------+--------+
| name           | price | weight |
+----------------+-------+--------+
| Small product  |  5.99 |   1.50 |
| Medium product |  9.99 |   4.50 |
| Large product  | 15.99 |   8.00 |
+----------------+-------+--------+
3 rows in set (0.00 sec)
```

Formatting Queries   In the examples in this book, queries are formatted so that each clause of a SQL statement is on a separate line. The formatting does not affect the operation of a SQL statement; you can use carriage returns and whitespace to format a query however you want.

Although it might seem excessive to adopt a formatting style for these simple examples, as you add more clauses to a query and learn to build more complex SQL statements in subsequent lessons, formatting your queries in a readable way becomes very important.

Retrieving All Columns

If you want to retrieve the data from every column in a table, you do not need to specify each column name after the SELECT keyword. Use the asterisk character (*) in place of a column list in a SELECT statement to instruct MySQL to return every column from the specified table.

The following query retrieves every column and row from the products table:

```
mysql> SELECT *
    -> FROM products;
+------+----------------+--------+-------+
| code | name           | weight | price |
+------+----------------+--------+-------+
| MINI | Small product  |   1.50 |  5.99 |
| MIDI | Medium product |   4.50 |  9.99 |
| MAXI | Large product  |   8.00 | 15.99 |
+------+----------------+--------+-------+
3 rows in set (0.00 sec)
```

Note that the output produced is exactly the same, as if you had specified each column in the query by name, like this:

```
mysql> SELECT code, name, weight, price
    -> FROM products;
+------+----------------+--------+-------+
| code | name           | weight | price |
+------+----------------+--------+-------+
| MINI | Small product  |   1.50 |  5.99 |
| MIDI | Medium product |   4.50 |  9.99 |
| MAXI | Large product  |   8.00 | 15.99 |
+------+----------------+--------+-------+
3 rows in set (0.00 sec)
```

When you use SELECT *, columns are displayed in the order they occur in the database table—the order in which columns were specified when the table was created. You will learn how to create database tables in Lesson 14, "Creating and Modifying Tables."

Compare the order of the columns in the result of the previous query to the output produced by the DESCRIBE command for products.

```
mysql> DESCRIBE products;
+---------+--------------+------+-----+---------+-------+
| Field   | Type         | Null | Key | Default | Extra |
+---------+--------------+------+-----+---------+-------+
| code    | varchar(10)  |      |     |         |       |
| name    | varchar(40)  |      |     |         |       |
| weight  | decimal(6,2) |      |     | 0.00    |       |
| price   | decimal(6,2) |      |     | 0.00    |       |
+---------+--------------+------+-----+---------+-------+
4 rows in set (0.00 sec)
```

 Query Results   The tabular layout that mysql produces when displaying the results of a query is a simple yet readable format for viewing small amounts of data. However, your screen has only a fixed width, so if you try to display too many columns—or if a SELECT * returns a lot of columns—the characters that make up this table could wrap lines and create an unreadable mess.

Mistakes in a SELECT Statement

Before long, you will mistype a SELECT statement—if you have not done so already! Here you look at some of the error messages MySQL gives when you make a mistake.

If you try to select data from a table that does not exist, MySQL gives an error message. In this example, you attempted to select from a table named product instead of products:

```
mysql> SELECT *
    -> FROM product;
ERROR 1146 (42S02): Table sampdb.product' doesn't exist
```

If you specify a column name that does not exist in the selected table, you will see the following error message:

```
mysql> SELECT name
    -> FROM customer_contacts;
ERROR 1054 (42S22): Unknown column 'name' in 'field list'
```

In this case, the `customer_contacts` table does not have a `name` column—it has separate `first_name` and `last_name` columns.

 Case Sensitivity MySQL table names are case sensitive, but column names are not. A table named `Products` is different than `products`, and executing `SELECT * FROM Products` will produce an error in the sample database. However, specifying the `name` column as `Name` or `NAME` will not cause an error.

If you make a syntax error—that is, when MySQL cannot understand the `SELECT` statement because things do not appear in the order that it expects them to—the error message looks like the following:

```
mysql> SELECT first_name, last name,
    -> FROM customer_contacts;
ERROR 1064 (42000): You have an error in your SQL syntax; check
the manual that corresponds to your MySQL server version for
the right syntax to use near 'FROM customer_contacts' at line 2
```

In the previous example, note the comma after `last_name`. When MySQL sees this, it expects another column name to follow, but instead the next word is `FROM`. Because you cannot use a SQL keyword as a column name, this causes the syntax error as shown.

MySQL can also throw up a syntax error if you misspell a keyword. In the following example, the keyword `FROM` was mistyped as `FORM`. The error displayed indicates that MySQL does not know what purpose the word `FORM` serves in the SQL statement, so it cannot execute this query.

```
mysql> SELECT name
    -> FORM products;
ERROR 1064 (42000): You have an error in your SQL syntax; check
the manual that corresponds to your MySQL server version for
the right syntax to use near 'products' at line 2
```

Multiple Errors   If there are several errors in your query, MySQL will tell you only about the first one that it encounters. Of the three error types shown previously, MySQL will report a syntax error first, followed by a nonexistent table and finally a bad column name.

Consider the error in the following statement, in which you mistyped a two-word column name by leaving out the underscore character in the name. MySQL does not allow column names to contain a space, so an underscore is often used to separate words.

```
mysql> SELECT first_name, last name
    -> FROM customer_contacts;
ERROR 1054 (42S22): Unknown column 'last' in 'field list'
```

In this example, MySQL gives an unknown column error instead of a syntax error. The actual way MySQL interprets this is to select a column named `last` and give it an alias `name`, so there's actually no error in the statement syntax. Don't worry about the details of this for now—it's covered in Lesson 12, "Creating Advanced Joins."

 Semantic Errors   The previous error is an example of a semantic error. The statement syntax is technically correct and is accepted by the MySQL interpreter, but the actual meaning of the statement is not what you intended it to be.

Retrieving Database Information

To construct a valid `SELECT` statement, you need to know how a database is organized. The `SHOW` command is used to retrieve information about database components.

Retrieving a List of Databases

Use the SHOW DATABASES command to retrieve a list of databases that you have access to. Execute the SHOW command just like a SELECT statement from the mysql program.

```
mysql> SHOW DATABASES;
+-------------------+
| Database          |
+-------------------+
| mysqlin10         |
| mydb              |
+-------------------+
2 rows in set (0.00 sec)
```

Retrieving a List of Tables

When you have connected to a database with the use command in mysql, you can obtain a list of tables in that database with the SHOW TABLES command.

```
mysql> SHOW TABLES;
+---------------------+
| Tables_in_mysqlin10 |
+---------------------+
| customer_contacts   |
| customers           |
| order_lines         |
| orders              |
| products            |
+---------------------+
5 rows in set (0.00 sec)
```

If you are connected to one database but want to list the tables in another, you can use a FROM clause with SHOW TABLES.

```
mysql> SHOW TABLES FROM sampdb;
+---------------------+
| Tables_in_sambdb    |
+---------------------+
| customer_contacts   |
| customers           |
| order_lines         |
| orders              |
| products            |
+---------------------+
5 rows in set (0.00 sec)
```

Retrieving a List of Columns

To retrieve the table structure for a database table, use the SHOW COLUMNS command using the table name in the FROM clause.

```
mysql> SHOW COLUMNS FROM products;
+--------+--------------+------+-----+---------+-------+
| Field  | Type         | Null | Key | Default | Extra |
+--------+--------------+------+-----+---------+-------+
| code   | varchar(10)  |      |     |         |       |
| name   | varchar(40)  |      |     |         |       |
| weight | decimal(6,2) |      |     | 0.00    |       |
| price  | decimal(6,2) |      |     | 0.00    |       |
+--------+--------------+------+-----+---------+-------+
4 rows in set (0.00 sec)
```

Describe   The DESCRIBE command is a shortcut for the SHOW COLUMNS command; DESCRIBE *table* is identical to SHOW COLUMNS FROM *table*.

Summary

In this lesson, you learned how to retrieve records from a database using a SELECT statement. In the next lesson, you will learn how to filter the results of a query and specify sorting on the data.

LESSON 4

Filtering and Sorting Data

In this lesson, you learn how to add a WHERE clause to a SELECT statement to filter the retrieved data, and how to use an ORDER BY clause to sort the query results.

The WHERE Clause

You can add a WHERE clause to a SELECT statement to tell MySQL to filter the query results based on a given rule. Rules in a WHERE clause refer to data values returned by the query, and only rows in which the values meet the criteria in the rule are returned.

Filtering on an Exact Value

The simplest type of filter in a WHERE clause uses the equals operator (=) to specify that a data value must match a given value exactly.

The following query retrieves all the contacts for a given company:

```
mysql> SELECT id, first_name, last_name
    -> FROM customer_contacts
    -> WHERE customer_code = 'SCICORP';
+----+------------+-----------+
| id | first_name | last_name |
+----+------------+-----------+
|  4 | Albert     | Einstein  |
|  5 | Charles    | Darwin    |
|  6 | Marie      | Curie     |
|  7 | Benjamin   | Franklin  |
+----+------------+-----------+
4 rows in set (0.03 sec)
```

In this example, rows from customer_contacts are returned only if the value of customer_code in that row is equal to SCICORP.

You often use an exact match operator in a WHERE clause to return all the columns in a table when you know the primary key of a record. For instance, to find all the information about a product from its unique product code, you could use the following query:

```
mysql> SELECT *
    -> FROM products
    -> WHERE code = 'MIDI';
+------+----------------+--------+-------+
| code | name           | weight | price |
+------+----------------+--------+-------+
| MIDI | Medium product |   4.50 |  9.99 |
+------+----------------+--------+-------+
1 row in set (0.00 sec)
```

To perform a condition using an inequality, use the != operator. This works just the same as =, but the condition returns only rows in which the table value is not equal to the value given in the condition.

For instance, the following query finds all products except for MINI:

```
mysql> SELECT *
    -> FROM products
    -> WHERE code != 'MINI';
+------+----------------+--------+-------+
| code | name           | weight | price |
+------+----------------+--------+-------+
| MIDI | Medium product |   4.50 |  9.99 |
| MAXI | Large product  |   8.00 | 15.99 |
+------+----------------+--------+-------+
2 rows in set (0.02 sec)s
```

Filtering on a Range of Values

In addition to the equality operator, you can use a set of operators to select rows based on a range of values. Use the symbols < and > to test whether one value is less than or greater than another value, respectively.

When followed by an = symbol, these operators also match equal values. The symbol sequence >= means "is greater than or equal to," whereas <= means "is less than or equal to."

To find only products for which the price is $9.99 or lower, use the following query:

```
mysql> SELECT *
    -> FROM products
    -> WHERE price <= 9.99;
+------+----------------+--------+-------+
| code | name           | weight | price |
+------+----------------+--------+-------+
| MINI | Small product  |   1.50 |  5.99 |
| MIDI | Medium product |   4.50 |  9.99 |
+------+----------------+--------+-------+
2 rows in set (0.00 sec)
```

This example uses the <= operator, meaning that rows in which the price value is less than or equal to 9.99 are returned. If you use the < operator instead, the MIDI product will not be returned by the query because it costs exactly $9.99.

The range operators can be performed on textual data, and the results are logical. For example, performing a greater-than comparison on the last_name field returns only values that are alphabetically higher than the given value.

```
mysql> SELECT last_name
    -> FROM customer_contacts
    -> WHERE last_name > 'G';
+-----------+
| last_name |
+-----------+
| Lincoln   |
| Nixon     |
| Roosevelt |
| Gershwin  |
| Lennon    |
+-----------+
5 rows in set (0.00 sec)
```

Word Comparisons   Comparing text strings in MySQL works like the ordering of words in a dictionary. The word *sandwich* would appear after the word *sand* in the dictionary because it is a longer word. Similarly MySQL would consider *sandwich* to be a greater value than *sand.*

Using Quotes Around Values

You might have noticed in the previous examples that sometimes the values used in a WHERE clause were contained in single quotes. This is necessary when the value being compared is a non-numeric value because MySQL needs to know whether you are referring to a fixed value or a column name from a table in the query.

Consider the following query, which produces the error shown:

```
mysql> SELECT last_name
    -> FROM customer_contacts
    -> WHERE first_name = Benjamin;
ERROR 1054 (42S22): Unknown column 'Benjamin' in 'where clause'
```

The error message indicates that MySQL is trying to find a column named Benjamin in the customer_contacts table—of course, this does not exist. To tell MySQL that a value is not a column name, you must enclose it in quotes, as shown:

```
mysql> SELECT last_name
    -> FROM customer_contacts
    -> WHERE first_name = 'Benjamin';
+-----------+
| last_name |
+-----------+
| Franklin  |
| Britten   |
+-----------+
2 rows in set (0.00 sec)
```

Although the usual convention in a WHERE clause is WHERE *column* = '*value*', this ordering is not significant. The following query demonstrates that the order can be reversed without affecting the outcome:

```
mysql> SELECT last_name
    -> FROM customer_contacts
    -> WHERE 'Benjamin' = first_name;
+-----------+
| last_name |
+-----------+
| Franklin  |
| Britten   |
+-----------+
2 rows in set (0.00 sec)
```

Number Values   Quotes are not needed around number values. MySQL does not get confused with numeric comparisons because a column name cannot begin with a number.

MySQL does enable you to perform a query using two columns, although this is rarely useful with two columns from the same table. A slightly peculiar example is shown here:

```
mysql> SELECT first_name, last_name
    -> FROM customer_contacts
    -> WHERE first_name = last_name;
Empty set (0.00 sec)
```

This query attempts to find names from the `customer_contacts` table whose first name and last name are the same. Such names are unusual—the query will find only names such as Scott Scott or Thomas Thomas—so no rows are returned from the sample tables. Note that this query does not find matches for Benjamin Franklin and Franklin Roosevelt—it compares only the `first_name` and `last_name` values from a single row of data.

Comparing Column Values   Having two different column names on either side of the = character in a WHERE clause is an important SQL technique for queries that use more than one table. You will learn how to do this in Lesson 11, "Joining Tables."

The ORDER BY Clause

So far, you have seen that data is fetched from the database in no particular order. To specify the sorting on the result of a query, you can add an ORDER BY clause.

Sorting on a Single Column

The following example retrieves all the products in order of price. The keywords ORDER BY are followed by the name of the column on which you want to sort.

```
mysql> SELECT *
    -> FROM products
    -> ORDER BY price;
+------+----------------+--------+-------+
| code | name           | weight | price |
+------+----------------+--------+-------+
| MINI | Small product  |   1.50 |  5.99 |
| MIDI | Medium product |   4.50 |  9.99 |
| MAXI | Large product  |   8.00 | 15.99 |
+------+----------------+--------+-------+
3 rows in set (0.00 sec)
```

 Sort Columns   The sort column specified in ORDER BY does not actually have to appear in the list of columns after the SELECT keyword. You can, therefore, specify a sort order using a column that is not retrieved by the query.

When you want to add sorting to a query that is also filtered, the ORDER BY clause must appear after the WHERE clause. This example finds all the contacts for one customer sorted on the last name.

```
mysql> SELECT first_name, last_name
    -> FROM customer_contacts
    -> WHERE customer_code = 'SCICORP'
    -> ORDER BY last_name;
```

```
+-------------+-------------+
| first_name  | last_name   |
+-------------+-------------+
| Marie       | Curie       |
| Charles     | Darwin      |
| Albert      | Einstein    |
| Benjamin    | Franklin    |
+-------------+-------------+
4 rows in set (0.00 sec)
```

Sorting on Multiple Columns

The ORDER BY clause is formed in a similar way to the first line of a SELECT statement. If you want to specify a sort order that involves more than one column in the query, separate the column names with a comma.

The following query fetches data from the orders table in date order. The second sort column, customer_code, is used to specify the sorting when the values of order_date are the same.

```
mysql> SELECT order_date, customer_code
    -> FROM orders
    -> ORDER BY order_date, customer_code;
+-------------+---------------+
| order_date  | customer_code |
+-------------+---------------+
| 2006-01-23  | PRESINC       |
| 2006-01-23  | SCICORP       |
| 2006-01-26  | PRESINC       |
| 2006-02-01  | MUSGRP        |
| 2006-02-02  | MUSGRP        |
| 2006-02-02  | SCICORP       |
| 2006-02-05  | SCICORP       |
+-------------+---------------+
7 rows in set (0.00 sec)
```

Specifying Sort Order

By default, the ordering on a column specified in the ORDER BY clause is done in ascending order, either numerically or alphabetically, depending on the data type of the column.

To specify a descending sort direction, use the DESC keyword. The following example sorts the data from the products table with the heaviest at the top of the list.

```
mysql> SELECT *
    -> FROM products
    -> ORDER BY weight DESC;
+--------+-----------------+--------+-------+
| code   | name            | weight | price |
+--------+-----------------+--------+-------+
| MAXI   | Large product   |   8.00 | 15.99 |
| MIDI   | Medium product  |   4.50 |  9.99 |
| MINI   | Small product   |   1.50 |  5.99 |
+--------+-----------------+--------+-------+
3 rows in set (0.00 sec)
```

Ascending Order   To explicitly specify ascending sort order, use the ASC keyword in place of DESC. The ASC keyword is optional, but it can be useful to indicate the sort order clearly in a query.

Multiple Sort Orders   When you specify more than one sort column, the keywords ASC and DESC can be used after each column name. You must specify the order direction for each sort in turn.

Summary

In this lesson, you learned how to filter the rows returned by a SELECT statement using a WHERE clause. You also learned how to specify a sort order on the result of a query using ORDER BY. In the next lesson, you will learn how to perform more advanced data filtering on a query.

LESSON 5
Advanced Data Filtering

In this lesson, you learn about more conditional operators that can be used in a WHERE clause. You also learn how to combine conditions to perform more advanced filtering on a query.

Combining WHERE Clauses

The examples you have seen so far perform filtering on a query based on only a single condition. To provide greater control over a result set, MySQL enables you to combine a number of conditions in a WHERE clause. They are joined using the logical operator keywords AND and OR.

Using the AND Operator

After adding a WHERE clause to filter a query, you can filter the results further by adding another condition with the AND operator.

This is commonly used to restrict the query results based on the values of two or more columns, as shown in the following example:

```
mysql> SELECT * FROM orders
    -> WHERE customer_code = 'SCICORP'
    -> AND order_date >= '2006-02-01';
+----+---------------+------------+
| id | customer_code | order_date |
+----+---------------+------------+
|  4 | SCICORP       | 2006-02-02 |
|  5 | SCICORP       | 2006-02-05 |
+----+---------------+------------+
2 rows in set (0.00 sec)
```

This query returns only rows from the orders table in which both conditions hold true. The customer_code must be SCICORP, and the order_date must be on or after February 1, 2006.

AND   For a query row to be returned, the table data in question must satisfy all the conditions separated by an AND operator. If any one condition fails for a record, that record is filtered out.

Using the OR Operator

Whereas the AND operator specifies a filter that further restricts the number of rows returned by a query, the OR operator is used to relax the filtering criteria by specifying alternative filter conditions. If one or more of the conditions separated by an OR operator hold true for a row in the table, that record will appear in the query results.

The following example shows the same example you saw for the AND operator, but using an OR instead:

```
mysql> SELECT * FROM orders
    -> WHERE customer_code = 'SCICORP'
    -> OR order_date >= '2006-02-01';
+----+---------------+------------+
| id | customer_code | order_date |
+----+---------------+------------+
|  3 | SCICORP       | 2006-01-23 |
|  4 | SCICORP       | 2006-02-02 |
|  5 | SCICORP       | 2006-02-05 |
|  6 | MUSGRP        | 2006-02-01 |
|  7 | MUSGRP        | 2006-02-02 |
+----+---------------+------------+
5 rows in set (0.00 sec)
```

The result set for this query includes all orders for SCICORP, regardless of order_date, as well as any orders for other customers that were placed on or after February 1.

OR   For a query row to be returned, the table data in question must satisfy at least one of the conditions separated by an OR operator. Every condition must fail for a record to be filtered out.

This example finds all the customers who have the name Franklin, whether that is their first name or last name:

```
mysql> SELECT first_name, last_name
    -> FROM customer_contacts
    -> WHERE first_name = 'Franklin'
    -> OR last_name = 'Franklin';
+------------+-----------+
| first_name | last_name |
+------------+-----------+
| Franklin   | Roosevelt |
| Benjamin   | Franklin  |
+------------+-----------+
2 rows in set (0.00 sec)
```

Filtering on Multiple Values

You could use the OR operator with equals conditions to specify multiple filter values for the same column. For instance, the following query finds all the customer contacts called either Benjamin or Charles:

```
mysql> SELECT first_name, last_name
    -> FROM customer_contacts
    -> WHERE first_name = 'Benjamin'
    -> OR first_name = 'Charles';
+------------+-----------+
| first_name | last_name |
+------------+-----------+
| Charles    | Darwin    |
| Benjamin   | Franklin  |
| Benjamin   | Britten   |
+------------+-----------+
3 rows in set (0.00 sec)
```

However, because this is a relatively common type of filter, there is a handy shortcut. You can use the IN operator to perform exactly this type of filter in a single condition. IN works like multiple equals operators and takes a comma-separated list of values, enclosed in parentheses.

Brackets   The proper name for the brackets used in MySQL is *parentheses*. Because MySQL uses only parentheses, however, you can refer to them as brackets without confusing them with square brackets or braces.

The following query is equivalent to the previous example:

```
mysql> SELECT first_name, last_name
    -> FROM customer_contacts
    -> WHERE first_name IN ('Benjamin', 'Charles');
+------------+-----------+
| first_name | last_name |
+------------+-----------+
| Charles    | Darwin    |
| Benjamin   | Franklin  |
| Benjamin   | Britten   |
+------------+-----------+
3 rows in set (0.00 sec)
```

You can already see that this query is more concise and easier to read when you use IN. Imagine how cumbersome a query would become without it if you had to use the OR operator with a long list of values to compare.

Instead of matching against a list of values, the BETWEEN operator enables you to search for data within a given range. It takes two target values separated by the keyword AND. Rows in which the column data is between—and including—those values are returned. The following example finds only orders placed in a given week in January:

```
mysql> SELECT *
    -> FROM orders
    -> WHERE order_date BETWEEN '2006-01-24' AND '2006-01-30';
+----+---------------+------------+
| id | customer_code | order_date |
+----+---------------+------------+
|  2 | PRESINC       | 2006-01-26 |
|  3 | SCICORP       | 2006-01-23 |
+----+---------------+------------+
2 rows in set (0.00 sec)
```

Date Comparisons   The previous example used the BETWEEN operator to compare two dates. In MySQL, dates are compared as numeric values, with earlier dates having lower values than later dates. You will learn more about date values in MySQL in Lesson 8, "Date Operators and Functions."

Negating a Condition

Using the NOT keyword negates a condition—it makes it behave in the opposite way.

A powerful use of NOT is the NOT IN condition. Instead of specifying a list of values that a column value should match, you specify a list of values that should be excluded from the query result.

The following query finds customers from a given company code but also excludes a list of names from the result:

```
mysql> SELECT first_name, last_name FROM customer_contacts
    -> WHERE customer_code = 'PRESINC'
    -> AND first_name NOT IN ('Abraham', 'Theodore');
+------------+-----------+
| first_name | last_name |
+------------+-----------+
| Richard    | Nixon     |
| Franklin   | Roosevelt |
+------------+-----------+
2 rows in set (0.00 sec)
```

Similarly, you can use the NOT operator with a BETWEEN statement to exclude a range of values from the query result. The following example finds only orders that were placed outside the period given:

```
mysql> SELECT * FROM orders
    -> WHERE order_date NOT BETWEEN '2006-01-26' AND
➥'2006-02-03';
+----+---------------+------------+
| id | customer_code | order_date |
+----+---------------+------------+
```

```
|  1 | PRESINC        | 2006-01-23 |
|  3 | SCICORP        | 2006-01-23 |
|  5 | SCICORP        | 2006-02-05 |
+----+----------------+------------+
3 rows in set (0.00 sec)
```

Operator Precedence

Consider the following query, which contains both an AND and an OR operator:

```
mysql> SELECT customer_code, first_name, last_name
    -> FROM customer_contacts
    -> WHERE customer_code = 'SCICORP'
    -> AND first_name = 'Albert'
    -> OR first_name = 'Benjamin';
```

Before looking at the output from this query, try to determine what MySQL is actually looking for here. This query could filter the customer contact data in two possible ways.

You might expect that the query would return contacts for the company SCICORP with one of the first names given. Or you might think that it will return anyone named Albert from SCICORP, as well as any other contact named Benjamin. However, unless you know whether MySQL assigns more importance to an AND or an OR, you will not be able to say for sure without running the query.

The actual results from the previous query are shown here:

```
+---------------+------------+-----------+
| customer_code | first_name | last_name |
+---------------+------------+-----------+
| SCICORP       | Albert     | Einstein  |
| SCICORP       | Benjamin   | Franklin  |
| MUSGRP        | Benjamin   | Britten   |
+---------------+------------+-----------+
3 rows in set (0.00 sec)
```

As you can see, a Benjamin from a company other than SCICORP appears in the results. This is because MySQL treats an AND with higher *precedence* than an OR. The effect is that the conditions on either side of the AND are evaluated first, before the OR operator is considered.

Precedence The order in which components of SQL statements are evaluated is called precedence. For conditional operators, AND has a higher precedence than OR, which, in turn, has a higher precedence than NOT.

To override the natural order of evaluation, you can put parentheses around conditions to indicate that they should be evaluated together. The following query uses parentheses to override the operator precedence of the previous example:

```
mysql> SELECT customer_code, first_name, last_name
    -> FROM customer_contacts
    -> WHERE customer_code = 'SCICORP'
    -> AND (first_name = 'Albert'
    -> OR first_name = 'Benjamin');
+---------------+------------+-----------+
| customer_code | first_name | last_name |
+---------------+------------+-----------+
| SCICORP       | Albert     | Einstein  |
| SCICORP       | Benjamin   | Franklin  |
+---------------+------------+-----------+
2 rows in set (0.00 sec)
```

This time, the two queries on either side of the OR operator are evaluated first, before the AND operator is considered. This query returns a row only if the customer_code condition is true and at least one of the conditions in the OR is met.

Using Parentheses You can use parentheses to indicate the order of evaluation even if doing so will not affect the natural operator precedence. This will make your queries more readable.

Limiting the Number of Rows Returned

If you are expecting a query to still return more rows that you want, even with the filtering from a WHERE clause applied, you can add a LIMIT clause to specify the maximum number of records to be returned.

Using a LIMIT Clause

The following example retrieves all the rows from the customer_ contacts table, but the LIMIT clause restricts the number of rows returned to three:

```
mysql> SELECT first_name, last_name
    -> FROM customer_contacts
    -> ORDER BY last_name
    -> LIMIT 3;
+------------+-----------+
| first_name | last_name |
+------------+-----------+
| Benjamin   | Britten   |
| Marie      | Curie     |
| Charles    | Darwin    |
+------------+-----------+
3 rows in set (0.00 sec)
```

 Limiting Sorted Records   The sorting specified in an ORDER BY clause is performed as if the full result of the query was fetched, regardless of the number of rows specified by the LIMIT clause.

By specifying sorting on a query column and using a LIMIT clause to limit the number of rows returned to just one, you can tell MySQL to return only the record with the highest or lowest value in that column. The following example returns only the most expensive product from the products table, by sorting price in descending order:

```
mysql> SELECT *
    -> FROM products
    -> ORDER BY price DESC
    -> LIMIT 1;
+------+----------------+--------+-------+
| code | name           | weight | price |
+------+----------------+--------+-------+
| MAXI | Large product  |   8.00 | 15.99 |
+------+----------------+--------+-------+
1 row in set (0.00 sec)
```

Skipping Rows

If the LIMIT clause contains two numbers separated by a comma, the first is an offset argument and the second is the number of rows to return. The offset specifies the number of rows to skip before returning the first record.

The next two queries show this in action. First select all the customers' email addresses in alphabetical order and show just the first three rows.

```
mysql> SELECT email
    -> FROM customer_contacts
    -> ORDER BY email
    -> LIMIT 3;
+--------------------------+
| email                    |
+--------------------------+
| britten@musgrp.com       |
| curie@sciencecorp.com    |
| darwin@sciencecorp.com   |
+--------------------------+
3 rows in set (0.00 sec)
```

The next query uses an offset value to show the next three rows from the query result.

```
mysql> SELECT email
    -> FROM customer_contacts
    -> ORDER BY email
    -> LIMIT 3,3;
+--------------------------+
| email                    |
+--------------------------+
| einstein@sciencecorp.com |
| fdr@presidentsinc.com    |
| franklin@sciencecorp.com |
+--------------------------+
3 rows in set (0.00 sec)
```

Notice that there is no overlap here—the offset value of 3 causes the fourth, fifth, and sixth rows of the query result to be displayed.

 Skipping Rows   Remember that the offset value in a LIMIT clause is the number of rows to skip, not the number of the first row to display. LIMIT 5 is equivalent to LIMIT 0,5—not LIMIT 1,5.

Summary

In this lesson, you learned how to use AND and OR to add more conditions to a WHERE clause. You also learned how to restrict the number of rows returned by a query, using LIMIT.

LESSON 6

Numeric Operators and Functions

In this lesson, you learn about the numeric operators and functions that are available in MySQL, allowing you to perform operations from basic arithmetic to complex mathematics.

Numeric Operators

In Lesson 4, "Filtering and Sorting Data," you saw how the comparison operators in MySQL were used to restrict the number of rows returned by a query.

Numeric operators are used in a similar way—two values appear on either side of a symbol or a sequence of symbols. This expression equates to a new value in the SQL statement.

 Operators and Operands In the expression a + b, the + symbol is the *operator* and a and b are known as *operands*.

Using Arithmetic Operators

An expression that uses a numeric operator can be used in a SQL statement anywhere that you could otherwise put a numeric value. You can also use a numeric operator to modify retrieved data from a table, as long as it is numeric data.

You can actually perform a query in MySQL without supplying a table name. This is useful only when you have an expression as a selected value, but it can be used to show the result of an expression on fixed values.

Addition in MySQL is performed using the + operator, and subtraction using the - operator. The following query shows an expression using each of these operators:

```
mysql> SELECT 15 + 28, 94 - 55;
+---------+---------+
| 15 + 28 | 94 - 55 |
+---------+---------+
|      43 |      39 |
+---------+---------+
1 row in set (0.00 sec)
```

A query with no table list returns exactly one row but can contain multiple columns. In this example, the two columns returned contain the results of the two expressions in the SELECT statement.

The other basic arithmetic operators in MySQL are * and /, for multiplication and division, respectively. The / operator in MySQL returns a decimal number—it does not truncate the result or round it to the nearest whole number.

```
mysql> SELECT 6 * 8, 72 / 9, 2 / 3;
+-------+--------+-------+
| 6 * 8 | 72 / 9 | 2 / 3 |
+-------+--------+-------+
|    48 |   8.00 |  0.67 |
+-------+--------+-------+
1 row in set (0.00 sec)
```

Precedence   The *, /, DIV, and MOD operators have a higher precedence than + and -. You can use parentheses where necessary to alter the order in which an expression is evaluated.

The DIV operator can be used to perform division where only a whole number is returned and any remainder is simply discarded. The modulo operator is used to find the remainder after division and is performed using MOD or the % symbol.

The following query divides 20 by 3; the result is 6 with a remainder of 2.

```
mysql> SELECT 20 DIV 3, 20 % 3;
+----------+--------+
| 20 DIV 3 | 20 % 3 |
+----------+--------+
|        6 |      2 |
+----------+--------+
1 row in set (0.00 sec)
```

Calculated Columns

In the following example, the query retrieves price data from the products table. The third column contains an expression that applies a fixed discount to the price of each item.

```
mysql> SELECT code, price, price - 1.50
    -> FROM products;
+------+-------+--------------+
| code | price | price - 1.50 |
+------+-------+--------------+
| MINI |  5.99 |         4.49 |
| MIDI |  9.99 |         8.49 |
| MAXI | 15.99 |        14.49 |
+------+-------+--------------+
3 rows in set (0.00 sec)
```

The expression is evaluated for each row in the result set, and the calculated value is returned in its own column.

Notice that the heading of the calculated column shows the expression in full. If the column value is calculated as the result of a long expression, this could make the query output much too wide. If you want to give this column its own name, you can use the AS keyword to specify a column *alias*.

In the following example, sales tax of 10% is calculated by multiplying the database price by 0.1 using the multiplication operator, *. The calculated column is given an alias tax.

```
mysql> SELECT code, price, price * 0.1 AS tax
    -> FROM products;
+------+-------+------+
| code | price | tax  |
+------+-------+------+
| MINI |  5.99 | 0.60 |
| MIDI |  9.99 | 1.00 |
| MAXI | 15.99 | 1.60 |
+------+-------+------+
3 rows in set (0.02 sec)
```

 Column Aliases In addition to making the column headings more readable in the mysql program, aliases are required when you want to refer to a column by name in your application. By giving a column an alias in your query, you also make it identifiable to a programming language that can interface with MySQL. You will learn how various programming languages can fetch data from a MySQL database in Part VI, "Interfacing with MySQL."

NULL Values

If a database column does not contain any data, this is represented in MySQL as NULL. A NULL is no value—it is not the same as zero.

If you perform any kind of arithmetic in which one of the arguments is NULL, the result will also be NULL, as shown in the following example:

```
mysql> SELECT 10 + NULL, 10 / NULL, 10 % NULL;
+-----------+-----------+-----------+
| 10 + NULL | 10 / NULL | 10 % NULL |
+-----------+-----------+-----------+
|      NULL |      NULL |      NULL |
+-----------+-----------+-----------+
1 row in set (0.00 sec)
```

Checking for NULL   If you want to check for NULL in a query, use IS NULL or IS NOT NULL. Comparing *column* = NULL does not work.

Numeric Functions

A function is a MySQL command used in an SQL statement that takes one or more arguments and returns a value based on the values supplied. Just as with expressions, you can use a function anywhere a fixed value could otherwise be used, or to manipulate the value returned in a database column.

Case Sensitivity   Function names are not case sensitive in MySQL. For example, you can use ROUND(), Round(), or round()—these all perform the same function call.

Arguments   To pass a function more than one argument, separate the values in parentheses using a comma. If a function does not require any arguments, the parentheses must still be given—for instance, RAND().

Random Numbers

To generate a random number, use the RAND() function with no arguments. The result is a random decimal number between 0 and 1.

```
mysql> SELECT RAND(), RAND();
+------------------+------------------+
| RAND()           | RAND()           |
+------------------+------------------+
| 0.96684006784748 | 0.27750918760664 |
+------------------+------------------+
1 row in set (0.00 sec)
```

In the previous example, two different calls to RAND() caused two different random numbers to be generated; a different value is returned each time RAND() is called, even within the same query.

Shuffling a Query   You can use the RAND() function in an ORDER BY clause to shuffle the order in which records are returned. Simply use ORDER BY RAND(); the value of RAND() will be different for each row returned by the query, and the results will be sorted randomly according to this value.

An optional argument to RAND() specifies the random number seed. This resets the random number generator to a particular point in its sequence. Whenever the sequence is reset to a known point, the same sequence of random numbers will be generated.

Random Seeds   You should never need to seed the random number generator with an argument to RAND(). Calling the function without an argument will give a number that can be considered random.

Rounding Functions

This set of functions enables you to round decimal numbers in a particular way. Each of these functions takes a single decimal number argument and returns an integer result.

Decimals and Integers   In this book, we refer to whole numbers as *integers* and fractional numbers as *decimals*. These terms correspond to the MySQL column data types, which you will learn about in Lesson 14, "Creating and Modifying Tables."

The ROUND() function rounds a value up or down to the nearest integer.

```
mysql> SELECT ROUND(29.21), ROUND(32.76);
+--------------+--------------+
| ROUND(29.21) | ROUND(32.76) |
+--------------+--------------+
|           29 |           33 |
+--------------+--------------+
1 row in set (0.00 sec)
```

If you supply a second argument, the number will be rounded to that amount of decimal places instead of an integer.

```
mysql> SELECT ROUND(29.21, 1), ROUND(32.76, 1);
+-----------------+-----------------+
| ROUND(29.21, 1) | ROUND(32.76, 1) |
+-----------------+-----------------+
|            29.2 |            32.8 |
+-----------------+-----------------+
1 row in set (0.00 sec)
```

The CEILING and FLOOR functions round a decimal number up and down to the nearest integer, respectively.

```
mysql> SELECT CEILING(29.21), FLOOR(29.21);
+----------------+--------------+
| CEILING(29.21) | FLOOR(29.21) |
+----------------+--------------+
|             30 |           29 |
+----------------+--------------+
1 row in set (0.00 sec)
```

Rounding Negatives Rounding a negative number up produces a higher—that is, less negative—value. Rounding down produces a lower value. For instance, CEILING(-2.6) returns -2, not -3 because -2 is a numerically greater value than -2.6.

The TRUNCATE function takes two arguments, a number and a precision. It does not round the number, but simply removes from it decimal places in excess of the precision specified.

```
mysql> SELECT TRUNCATE(12.34567, 3);
+-----------------------+
| TRUNCATE(12.34567, 3) |
+-----------------------+
|                12.345 |
+-----------------------+
1 row in set (0.00 sec)
```

Mathematical Functions

This set of functions enables you to perform mathematical operations in a query.

To raise a number to a power, use the POW() function. It takes two arguments: POW(a,b) raises a to the power b.

```
mysql> SELECT POW(2,2), POW(2,3), POW(2,4);
+----------+----------+----------+
| POW(2,2) | POW(2,3) | POW(2,4) |
+----------+----------+----------+
|        4 |        8 |       16 |
+----------+----------+----------+
1 row in set (0.00 sec)
```

To find the square root of a number, use SQRT() with a single argument. The following example also shows how functions can be nested by putting one function call as the argument to another. It calculates the square root of a number after it has just been squared.

```
mysql> SELECT SQRT(POW(8,2));
+-----------------+
| SQRT(POW(8, 2)) |
+-----------------+
|               8 |
+-----------------+
1 row in set (0.00 sec)
```

To find the logarithm of a number, use the LOG( ) function. With one argument, a natural logarithm (base e) is returned. The opposite of LOG( ) is EXP( )—natural log base e is raised to the power given in the argument.

In the following example, the first column shows the value of e. The second column performs a natural logarithm on this value.

```
mysql> SELECT EXP(1), LOG(EXP(1));
+-----------------+-------------+
| EXP(1)          | LOG(EXP(1)) |
+-----------------+-------------+
| 2.718281828459  |           1 |
+-----------------+-------------+
1 row in set (0.00 sec)
```

When called with two arguments, the LOG( ) function uses the first argument as its base. For instance, LOG(10,*num*) returns the logarithm of *num* to base 10.

Trigonometry Functions

MySQL supports trigonometry functions to calculate the sine, cosine, and tangent of a value using SIN( ), COS( ), and TAN( ), respectively.

The argument to these functions should be a value in radians. The following examples use PI( )to supply arguments to these functions that are based on [pi].

```
mysql> SELECT SIN(PI()/2), COS(2*PI()), TAN(PI()/4);
+-------------+-------------+-------------+
| SIN(PI()/2) | COS(2*PI()) | TAN(PI()/4) |
+-------------+-------------+-------------+
|           1 |           1 |           1 |
+-------------+-------------+-------------+
1 row in set (0.00 sec)
```

Inverse Functions   The inverse functions for SIN(), COS(), and TAN() are ASIN(), ACOS(), and ATAN(), respectively. A valid result will be returned only for arguments between –1 and +1.

To convert a value in degrees to radians, use DEGREES(). Likewise, to convert radians to degrees, use RADIANS().

```
mysql> SELECT DEGREES(PI()/2), RADIANS(180);
+-----------------+------------------+
| DEGREES(PI()/2) | RADIANS(180)     |
+-----------------+------------------+
|              90 | 3.1415926535898  |
+-----------------+------------------+
1 row in set (0.00 sec)
```

Conditional Functions

MySQL also includes a set of functions that return their result based on a condition, just like the conditions you use in a WHERE clause.

TRUE and FALSE

Every condition returns a value, TRUE or FALSE, depending on whether the condition is satisfied. There is no Boolean data type in MySQL—TRUE equates to 1, and FALSE equates to 0.

You can actually see these values by executing a condition as a query, as follows:

```
mysql> SELECT code, price, price > 10.00
    -> FROM products;
+------+-------+---------------+
| code | price | price > 10.00 |
+------+-------+---------------+
| MINI |  5.99 |             0 |
| MIDI |  9.99 |             0 |
| MAXI | 15.99 |             1 |
+------+-------+---------------+
3 rows in set (0.00 sec)
```

The output from this query shows each product and its price from the products table. The conditional column returns TRUE when the price is greater than 10.00.

The IF() Function

The IF() function provides a way to return a value based on a condition within a query.

The first argument is a condition that is evaluated for each row of the query. The value in the second is returned if the condition is TRUE, and the third argument is returned if it is FALSE.

The following example is a very simple shipping rate calculator. If the product weight is less than 5 pounds, shipping costs $1.99; otherwise, it costs $2.99.

```
mysql> SELECT code, weight, IF(weight < 5, 1.99, 2.99)
    -> FROM products;
+------+--------+----------------------------+
| code | weight | IF(weight < 5, 1.99, 2.99) |
+------+--------+----------------------------+
| MINI |   1.50 |                       1.99 |
| MIDI |   4.50 |                       1.99 |
| MAXI |   8.00 |                       2.99 |
+------+--------+----------------------------+
3 rows in set (0.00 sec)
```

The CASE Statement

The CASE statement is a multiple-valued conditional construct. Suppose you wanted to set three or more shipping rates based on weight. This would require a complex series of nested IF() functions.

The following example uses a CASE statement to determine the shipping rate based on three different weight bands:

```
mysql> SELECT code, weight,
    ->         CASE WHEN weight < 2 THEN 1.99
    ->              WHEN weight < 5 THEN 2.99
    ->              ELSE 4.99 END as shipping
    -> FROM products;
```

```
+------+--------+----------+
| code | weight | shipping |
+------+--------+----------+
| MINI |   1.50 |     1.99 |
| MIDI |   4.50 |     2.99 |
| MAXI |   8.00 |     4.99 |
+------+--------+----------+
3 rows in set (0.00 sec)
```

A CASE can contain as many WHEN clauses as you need (in this example, there are two) and an ELSE clause that specifies a default value. A CASE statement can grow quite large; you must use the END keyword to indicate that it has ended.

If one of the WHEN clauses contains a condition that is TRUE, its corresponding value, given after the keyword THEN, is returned. Otherwise, the ELSE value is returned.

MySQL examines the WHEN clauses in the order they appear. In this example, the first value returned from the database is 1.50, which satisfies both WHEN conditions (it is less than both 2 and 5), but only the value from the first clause is returned.

 ELSE   If no ELSE clause is specified, a CASE statement that does not match any of the WHEN clauses returns NULL.

The IFNULL() Function

The IFNULL() function provides a shortcut when you expect to see NULL values. If the first argument is NULL, the second argument is returned; otherwise, the first argument is returned unchanged.

```
mysql> SELECT IFNULL(NULL, 99), IFNULL(55, 99);
+------------------+----------------+
| IFNULL(NULL, 99) | IFNULL(0, 99)  |
+------------------+----------------+
| 99               |              0 |
+------------------+----------------+
1 row in set (0.00 sec)
```

This example reaffirms that NULL and zero are not the same value.

The NULLIF() Function

Use NULLIF() to return NULL when two values are the same. If the two expressions passed to NULLIF() are the same, the result is NULL; otherwise, the first argument is returned. The following query replaces the price of a product that costs $9.99 with NULL.

```
mysql> SELECT code, price, NULLIF(price, 9.99)
    -> FROM products;
+------+-------+---------------------+
| code | price | NULLIF(price, 9.99) |
+------+-------+---------------------+
| MINI | 5.99  |                5.99 |
| MIDI | 9.99  |                NULL |
| MAXI | 15.99 |               15.99 |
+------+-------+---------------------+
3 rows in set (0.00 sec)
```

Summary

In this lesson, you learned how to use numeric operators and some of the most useful numeric functions in MySQL. The complete list of functions can be found at http://dev.mysql.com/doc/refman/5.0/en/numeric-functions.html. In the next lesson, you will learn how to work with string data in MySQL.

LESSON 7

String Operators and Functions

In this lesson, you learn about the string operators and functions that are available in MySQL, allowing you to manipulate character data in a query.

Using Operators with Strings

In the previous lesson, you saw how arithmetic and comparison operations were performed on numeric values. Now you'll see the ways in which you can work with strings in MySQL.

 Strings A string is simply a collection of characters treated as a single data item, either returned from a database column that contains characters or enclosed in single quotes in a SQL statement.

Comparison Operators

The comparison operators you are already familiar with translate to string values in a logical way. The equals and not equals operators work almost as you would expect, but MySQL is not case sensitive when comparing characters.

The following query shows that MySQL produces search results on a string comparison even if the case of the text does not match:

```
mysql> SELECT first_name, last_name
    -> FROM customer_contacts
    -> WHERE first_name IN ('CHARLES', 'marie');
+------------+-----------+
| first_name | last_name |
+------------+-----------+
| Charles    | Darwin    |
| Marie      | Curie     |
+------------+-----------+
2 rows in set (0.00 sec)
```

To force a case-sensitive string comparison, use the BINARY operator to instruct MySQL to compare the characters in the string using their underlying ASCII values rather than just their letters.

For example, you know that the string abc will match ABC by default, as shown here:

```
mysql> SELECT 'abc' = 'ABC';
+---------------+
| 'abc' = 'ABC' |
+---------------+
|             1 |
+---------------+
1 row in set (0.00 sec)
```

However, if you add the BINARY keyword before the expression, the case of each character becomes important.

```
mysql> SELECT BINARY 'abc' = 'ABC';
+----------------------+
| BINARY 'abc' = 'ABC' |
+----------------------+
|                    0 |
+----------------------+
1 row in set (0.00 sec)
```

 BINARY **Ordering** When you use an ORDER BY clause on a string column, results are returned alphabetically, regardless of case. For case-sensitive ordering, use ORDER BY BINARY column.

The greater than and less than operators perform an alphabetical comparison between two strings. For instance, cat is a lower value than dog.

The following query selects data from the customer_contacts table based on a range of values using the BETWEEN operator:

```
mysql> SELECT first_name, last_name
    -> FROM customer_contacts
    -> WHERE first_name BETWEEN 'C' and 'J'
    -> ORDER BY first_name;
+-------------+------------+
| first_name  | last_name  |
+-------------+------------+
| Charles     | Darwin     |
| Franklin    | Roosevelt  |
| George      | Gershwin   |
+-------------+------------+
3 rows in set (0.00 sec)
```

Note that the result from this query does not include records with the first name John. Although the first letter falls within the specified range, John is considered a greater value than simply the letter J because it contains more characters.

Compare this to the following query with the range specified using two letters. This time, the John record is returned because it falls within the range CA to JZ.

```
mysql> SELECT first_name, last_name
    -> FROM customer_contacts
    -> WHERE first_name BETWEEN 'CA' and 'JZ'
    -> ORDER BY first_name;
+-------------+------------+
| first_name  | last_name  |
+-------------+------------+
| Charles     | Darwin     |
| Franklin    | Roosevelt  |
| George      | Gershwin   |
| John        | Lennon     |
+-------------+------------+
4 rows in set (0.00 sec)
```

ASCII Comparisons   Because the letters a to z have higher ASCII values than A to Z, a capital letter is considered a lower value than its lower-case equivalent if compared using the BINARY operator.

Wildcards

The LIKE operator works just like the = operator but enables you to specify wildcards in the string to be matched. An underscore character matches any single character, whereas the percent symbol matches any number of characters.

For instance, to find all the contacts that have a last name beginning with L, you can use the following query:

```
mysql> SELECT last_name
    -> FROM customer_contacts
    -> WHERE last_name LIKE 'L%';
+-----------+
| last_name |
+-----------+
| Lincoln   |
| Lennon    |
+-----------+
2 rows in set (0.00 sec)
```

Case Sensitivity   As with other string operators, LIKE is not case sensitive unless you also use the BINARY operator.

You can use more than one wildcard character in a condition, if desired. The following example finds only names that contain the r and end with in:

```
mysql> SELECT last_name
    -> FROM customer_contacts
    -> WHERE last_name LIKE '%r%in';
+-----------+
| last_name |
+-----------+
| Darwin    |
| Franklin  |
| Gershwin  |
+-----------+
3 rows in set (0.00 sec)
```

The underscore character matches exactly one character, so using it in a wildcard expression restricts the values that will be matched using the position of letters within a string instead of simply the occurrence of a letter.

Changing the previous example as follows returns only names that contain the letter r in the third position and also end with in. This time, Franklin is excluded from the results.

```
mysql> SELECT last_name
    -> FROM customer_contacts
    -> WHERE last_name LIKE '__r%in';
+-----------+
| last_name |
+-----------+
| Darwin    |
| Gershwin  |
+-----------+
2 rows in set (0.00 sec)
```

 NOT LIKE   Use NOT LIKE with a wildcard pattern to exclude matching records from the query result.

Type Conversion

The idea of performing arithmetic operations on strings is a peculiar one. Although you will probably never have cause to do this, it is important to understand how MySQL handles expressions when the arguments are the wrong data type.

When you try to treat a string as a number, MySQL does its best to convert the value into the closest numeric equivalent. For example, if you add two numbers that are contained in quotes, MySQL returns the correct integer result even though these values are strings.

```
mysql> SELECT '100' + 45;
+------------+
| '100' + 45 |
+------------+
|        145 |
+------------+
1 row in set (0.00 sec)
```

When non-numeric text appears after a number, this is simply dropped.

```
mysql> SELECT '100 apples' + '45 bananas';
+----------------------------+
| '100 apples' + '45 bananas' |
+----------------------------+
|                        145 |
+----------------------------+
1 row in set (0.00 sec)
```

However, if text appears before a number in a string, its value is zero.

```
mysql> SELECT 'USD 100' + 10;
+----------------+
| 'USD 100' + 10 |
+----------------+
|             10 |
+----------------+
1 row in set (0.00 sec)
```

If the string contains text between two numbers, only the first number is used. In the following example, the string actually contains a numeric expression. Note that this is not evaluated; only the first number in the string—in this case, 4—is taken into account.

```
mysql> SELECT '4 * 2' + 1;
+------------+
| '4 * 2' + 1 |
+------------+
|          5 |
+------------+
1 row in set (0.00 sec)
```

String Functions

MySQL includes many functions that can be used to manipulate strings. You learn the most useful functions in this section.

 String Functions   Refer to the online manual for the full list of string functions: http://dev.mysql.com/doc/refman/5.0/en/string-functions.html.

Concatenation

Joining two or more strings is known as concatenation. It is performed using the CONCAT() function.

```
mysql> SELECT CONCAT('exam', 'ple');
+-----------------------+
| CONCAT('exam', 'ple') |
+-----------------------+
| example               |
+-----------------------+
1 row in set (0.00 sec)
```

The CONCAT() function can accept more than two arguments and returns a single string made up of each argument, in turn. Consider the following example:

```
mysql> SELECT CONCAT('Catch', 'a', 'falling', 'star');
+-----------------------------------------+
| CONCAT('Catch', 'a', 'falling', 'star') |
+-----------------------------------------+
| Catchafallingstar                       |
+-----------------------------------------+
1 row in set (0.00 sec)
```

All the string arguments are concatenated, and the result is as shown. No spaces are included in the concatenated string unless they are contained in the string arguments themselves.

Often you will want to separate the concatenated values with a character. You can do so using the CONCAT_WS() function (the WS part stands for "with separator"), taking the separator character as the first argument.

Compare the output of the following to the previous example, in which `CONCAT_WS()` is used with a space character to separate the words in the result.

```
mysql> SELECT CONCAT_WS(' ', 'Catch', 'a', 'falling', 'star');
+-------------------------------------------------+
| CONCAT_WS(' ', 'Catch', 'a', 'falling', 'star') |
+-------------------------------------------------+
| Catch a falling star                            |
+-------------------------------------------------+
1 row in set (0.00 sec)
```

Concatenation   Some database systems enable you to perform concatenation using an operator—usually the + or || symbols. In MySQL, however, you must use the `CONCAT()` function.

Trimming and Padding Strings

Sometimes you will be working with strings that contain excess white-space characters. To trim space characters from the beginning or end of a string, use `LTRIM()` and `RTRIM()`. `LTRIM()` removes characters from the left side of the string, and `RTRIM()` from the right.

```
mysql> SELECT LTRIM('   MySQL'), RTRIM('MySQL   ');
+------------------+------------------+
| LTRIM('   MySQL') | RTRIM('MySQL   ') |
+------------------+------------------+
| MySQL            | MySQL            |
+------------------+------------------+
1 row in set (0.00 sec)
```

Trimming   In print, you cannot actually see that trailing space characters have been trimmed by `RTRIM()`—you'll just have to trust that they have!

The TRIM() function has a different syntax that enables you to trim other characters than whitespace from either—or both—ends of a string. The keywords LEADING, TRAILING, and BOTH are used to specify which part of the string to trim, as shown in the following examples:

```
mysql> SELECT TRIM(LEADING '/' FROM '/dev/null');
+------------------------------------+
| TRIM(LEADING '/' FROM '/dev/null') |
+------------------------------------+
| dev/null                           |
+------------------------------------+
1 row in set (0.00 sec)

mysql> SELECT TRIM(TRAILING '.' FROM 'To be continued...');
+----------------------------------------------+
| TRIM(TRAILING '.' FROM 'To be continued...') |
+----------------------------------------------+
| To be continued                              |
+----------------------------------------------+
1 row in set (0.00 sec)
```

The opposite of trimming a string is padding it. MySQL provides the LPAD() and RPAD() functions, which pad a string to a fixed length by inserting characters on the left and right sides, respectively.

The arguments are the string to pad, the required length, and the padding character. The following example shows RPAD() being used on a database column to pad the name to 10 characters using periods:

```
mysql> SELECT RPAD(last_name, 10, '.')
    -> FROM customer_contacts
    -> WHERE customer_code = 'SCICORP';
+-------------------------+
| RPAD(last_name, 10, '.') |
+-------------------------+
| Einstein..              |
| Darwin....              |
| Curie.....              |
| Franklin..              |
+-------------------------+
4 rows in set (0.00 sec)
```

Search and Replace

The LOCATE() function returns the position of a substring within a string. The value returned is the character position of the first occurrence of the substring within the string, or zero if it is not found. The LENGTH() function returns the total number of characters in a string.

The following query shows some of the email addresses in the customer_contacts table. The second column shows the character position of the @ sign in each address, and the third column shows the total length of the string.

```
mysql> SELECT email, LOCATE('@', email), LENGTH(email)
    -> FROM customer_contacts
    -> WHERE customer_code = 'PRESINC';
+----------------------------+--------------------+--------+
| email                      | LOCATE('@', email) | LENGTH |
+----------------------------+--------------------+--------+
| lincoln@presidentsinc.com  |                  8 |     25 |
| nixon@presidentsinc.com    |                  6 |     23 |
| fdr@presidentsinc.com      |                  4 |     21 |
| roosevelt@presidentsinc.com|                 10 |     27 |
+----------------------------+--------------------+--------+
4 rows in set (0.00 sec)
```

The REPLACE() function can be used to replace one substring with another within a string. In the following example, the @ sign in an email address is replaced by the word *at*.

```
mysql> SELECT email, REPLACE(email, '@', ' at ')
    -> FROM customer_contacts
    -> WHERE customer_code = 'PRESINC';
+----------------------------+-------------------------------------+
| email                      | REPLACE(email, '@', ' at ')         |
+----------------------------+-------------------------------------+
| lincoln@presidentsinc.com  | lincoln at presidentsinc.com        |
| nixon@presidentsinc.com    | nixon at presidentsinc.com          |
| fdr@presidentsinc.com      | fdr at presidentsinc.com            |
| roosevelt@presidentsinc.com| roosevelt at presidentsinc.com      |
+----------------------------+-------------------------------------+
4 rows in set (0.00 sec)
```

Breaking Up a String

To return only a fixed portion of a string, use SUBSTRING(). The arguments are a string, a character position, and a length. The portion of the string beginning at the position is returned, up to the maximum length given.

The following query returns product names from the database, up to a maximum of 10 characters:

```
mysql> SELECT SUBSTRING(name, 1, 10)
    -> FROM products;
+------------------------+
| SUBSTRING(name, 1, 10) |
+------------------------+
| Small prod             |
| Medium pro             |
| Large prod             |
+------------------------+
3 rows in set (0.00 sec)
```

 Substring Shortcuts   If you pass a negative position argument to SUBSTRING() it counts backward from the end of the string to find the start position.

If you omit the length argument, the substring returned is taken from the given start position to the end of the string.

SUBSTRING() is useful when you want to split a string based on fixed character positions. To split a string based on the actual character values within it, MySQL provides the SUBSTRING_INDEX() function, so you don't have to use a clumsy combination of SUBSTRING() and LOCATE().

SUBSTRING_INDEX() takes a string argument followed by a delimiter character and the number of parts to return. After you break up the string using the delimiter, that number of parts is returned as a single string.

The following example returns the suffix from an Internet domain name:

```
mysql> SELECT SUBSTRING_INDEX('www.samspublishing.com',
➥'.', -1);
+------------------------------------------------------+
| SUBSTRING_INDEX('www.samspublishing.com', '.', -1) |
+------------------------------------------------------+
| com                                                  |
+------------------------------------------------------+
1 row in set (0.00 sec)
```

 Delimiters   In the previous example, if you were sure that domain suffixes are always three characters long, you could use SUBSTRING() with a -3 start position. However, because the suffix might be .com, .name, .ca, and so on, the period delimiter must be used instead of a fixed character position.

Case Conversion

To convert a string to all lower or upper case, use LOWER() and UPPER(). The following example shows the same column value converted to both cases:

```
mysql> SELECT UPPER(name), LOWER(name)
    -> FROM customers;
+------------------------+------------------------+
| UPPER(name)            | LOWER(name)            |
+------------------------+------------------------+
| PRESIDENTS INCORPORATED | presidents incorporated |
| SCIENCE CORPORATION    | science corporation    |
| MUSICIANS OF AMERICA   | musicians of america   |
+------------------------+------------------------+
3 rows in set (0.00 sec)
```

No single function exists in MySQL to capitalize only the first letter of a string, as you might often want to do with a person's name. The following shows how you can nest functions, combining LOWER() and UPPER() with SUBSTRING() and CONCAT() to produce this result:

```
mysql> SELECT CONCAT(UPPER(SUBSTRING(name, 1, 1)),
    ->                 LOWER(SUBSTRING(name, 2))) as name
    -> FROM customers;
+------------------------+
| name                   |
+------------------------+
| Presidents incorporated |
| Science corporation    |
| Musicians of america   |
+------------------------+
3 rows in set (0.00 sec)
```

NULL and Strings

In the previous lesson, you learned that a NULL is no value and that it is not the same as the number zero. Using NULL in an expression always causes the result to be NULL.

Similar rules apply for strings: NULL is not equal to an empty string. The following example also shows that having a NULL argument to CONCAT() causes NULL to be returned, regardless of the other arguments:

```
mysql> SELECT CONCAT('Hello', NULL, 'World');
+------------------------------+
| CONCAT('Hello', NULL, 'World') |
+------------------------------+
| NULL                         |
+------------------------------+
1 row in set (0.00 sec)
```

Summary

In this lesson, you learned how to use wildcards and met some of the most useful string-manipulation functions in MySQL. In the next lesson, you will learn how to work with date and time values.

LESSON 8

Date Operators and Functions

In this lesson, you learn how to work with date values in MySQL.

Date Operators

In the previous lessons, you saw how various operators work with numeric and string values. Although you can use the comparison operators with date values in the same way as numbers and strings, you must use a special syntax to perform arithmetic on date values.

Representing Dates and Times

A date value in MySQL takes the format YYYY-MM-DD or YYYYMMDD. Times take the format HH:MM:SS or HHMMSS. Until stored to the database or passed as an argument to a date function, however, this value is simply a string representation of a given date.

 Date and Time   You can have both date and time components in a single value, represented in the format YYYY-MM-DD HH:MM:SS.

This format places the most significant value first and the least significant last. Consequently, comparisons between dates take place in a logical way. In the following example, MySQL is simply comparing two strings or two numbers:

```
mysql> SELECT '2005-31-12' < '2006-01-01', 20053112 < 20060101;
+----------------------------+----------------------+
| '2005-31-12' < '2006-01-01' | 20053112 < 20060101 |
+----------------------------+----------------------+
|                          1 |                    1 |
+----------------------------+----------------------+
```

However, using the addition and subtraction operators on a date represented in a string can cause unpredictable results. Remember from the previous lesson that MySQL tries to perform numeric operations on a string by taking only the first numbers that appear.

```
mysql> SELECT '2005-06-01' + 10;
+-------------------+
| '2005-06-01' + 10 |
+-------------------+
|              2015 |
+-------------------+
1 row in set (0.00 sec)
```

Even using the numeric format with no hyphens, the results are far from perfect. In the following example, adding 7 days to March 30 should return April 6. Instead, the result looks like an invalid date in March.

```
mysql> SELECT 20050330 + 7;
+--------------+
| 20050330 + 7 |
+--------------+
|     20050337 |
+--------------+
1 row in set (0.00 sec)
```

Date and Time Data

Even when values are stored to a database column that is declared as one of the date and time data types that you will learn about in Lesson 14, "Creating and Modifying Tables," you cannot perform direct arithmetic on those values.

In the sample database, the order_date column in the orders table is a date type column. The following example shows that arithmetic on those date values can still produce dates that do not exist.

Date Columns There is actually no date logic at the database level. The only restriction is that the value must be in one of the recognized formats. Therefore, it is entirely possible for a date such as February 30 to be stored in a MySQL date column.

```
mysql> SELECT customer_code, order_date, order_date + 10
    -> FROM orders
    -> WHERE customer_code = 'SCICORP';
+---------------+------------+----------------+
| customer_code | order_date | order_date + 10 |
+---------------+------------+----------------+
| SCICORP       | 2006-01-23 |       20060133 |
| SCICORP       | 2006-02-02 |       20060212 |
| SCICORP       | 2006-02-05 |       20060215 |
+---------------+------------+----------------+
3 rows in set (0.00 sec)
```

Date Arithmetic

To instruct MySQL to perform date arithmetic using the addition and sub-traction operators, you must use the INTERVAL keyword along with a unit of time.

The following example adds 7 days to December 30, 2005, using date arithmetic:

```
mysql> SELECT '2005-12-30' + INTERVAL 7 DAY;
+------------------------------+
| '2005-12-30' + INTERVAL 7 DAY |
+------------------------------+
| 2006-01-06                   |
+------------------------------+
1 row in set (0.00 sec)
```

As you can see in this example, the value returned is the correct date after adding 7 days to December 29, 2005—the year, month, and date values have all been affected.

Changing the INTERVAL value provides an easy way to add different units of time to a date value. For instance, without needing to know how many days are in a given month, you can add 1 month to the date as follows:

```
mysql> SELECT '2005-12-29' + INTERVAL 1 MONTH;
+---------------------------------+
| '2005-12-29' + INTERVAL 1 MONTH |
+---------------------------------+
| 2006-01-29                      |
+---------------------------------+
1 row in set (0.00 sec)
```

Time intervals can also be used. The following example shows that when the time is incremented past midnight, the day value is also incremented:

```
mysql> SELECT '2005-12-31 22:30' + INTERVAL 2 HOUR;
+--------------------------------------+
| '2005-12-31 22:30' + INTERVAL 2 HOUR |
+--------------------------------------+
| 2006-01-01 00:30:00                  |
+--------------------------------------+
1 row in set (0.00 sec)
```

Intervals   In these examples, the intervals used were 7 DAY and 2 HOUR rather than 7 DAYS and 2 HOURS. MySQL requires the unit keyword to be singular, regardless of English grammar rules.

Table 8.1 lists the unit values that can be used with the INTERVAL keyword.

TABLE 8.1   INTERVAL Unit Keywords for Date Arithmetic

Keyword
MICROSECOND
SECOND
MINUTE

continues

TABLE 8.1   Continued

Keyword
HOUR
DAY
WEEK
MONTH
QUARTER
YEAR

There are a number of compound INTERVAL unit keywords, made up of two of the keywords from Table 8.1 separated by an underscore. The following example adds 2 hours and 30 minutes to a date using the HOUR_MINUTE unit:

```
mysql> SELECT '2005-12-31 22:30' + INTERVAL '2 30' HOUR_MINUTE;
+----------------------------------------------------+
| '2005-12-31 22:30' + INTERVAL '2 30' HOUR_MINUTE |
+----------------------------------------------------+
| 2006-01-01 01:00:00                                |
+----------------------------------------------------+
1 row in set (0.00 sec)
```

Note that when using a compound unit, the two unit values must be enclosed in single quotes and separated using a space character.

Date Functions

MySQL includes a range of functions for manipulating date and time values. You learn the most useful functions in this section.

Date Functions   Refer to the online manual for the full list of date and time functions: http://dev.mysql.com/doc/refman/5.0/en/date-and-time-functions.html.

Returning the Current Date and Time

The MySQL function CURDATE() returns the current date; CURTIME()
returns the current time, as shown in the following example:

```
mysql> SELECT CURDATE(), CURTIME();
+------------+-----------+
| CURDATE()  | CURTIME() |
+------------+-----------+
| 2005-10-28 | 16:24:45  |
+------------+-----------+
1 row in set (0.01 sec)
```

The NOW() function returns the current date and time as a single value.

```
mysql> SELECT NOW();
+---------------------+
| NOW()               |
+---------------------+
| 2005-10-28 16:24:45 |
+---------------------+
1 row in set (0.00 sec)
```

The actual date and time value returned by these functions is determined
by your system's time zone setting. Running NOW() on two servers based
in different parts of the world returns two different values.

Time Zones

The time zone upon which all others are calculated is Coordinated
Universal Time, abbreviated to UTC. The time in Hawaii is 10 hours
behind UTC, written as UTC-10, whereas in Japan, the local time is
UTC+9. Daylight saving time can modify this further at certain times of
the year.

To return the current date and time using a UTC clock, use UTC_DATE()
and UTC_TIME(). To return a single date and time value, use UTC_
TIMESTAMP(). The output in the following example is from a MySQL
server based on the West Coast of the United States, which is UTC-8:

```
mysql> SELECT CURTIME(), UTC_TIME();
+-----------+------------+
| CURTIME() | UTC_TIME() |
+-----------+------------+
| 08:48:43  | 16:48:43   |
+-----------+------------+
1 row in set (0.00 sec)
```

You can use the CONVERT_TZ() function to convert a time from one time zone to another. Given a date value and two time zone names, CONVERT_TZ() returns the date converted from the first time zone to the second.

In the following example, the date is converted from Pacific Standard Time to Eastern Standard Time:

```
mysql> SELECT CONVERT_TZ('2004-01-01 12:00:00',
    ->                    'US/Pacific', 'US/Eastern');
+----------------------------------------------------------------+
| CONVERT_TZ('2004-01-01 12:00:00','US/Pacific','US/Eastern')    |
+----------------------------------------------------------------+
| 2004-01-01 15:00:00                                            |
+----------------------------------------------------------------+
1 row in set (0.00 sec)
```

 Time Zones Not all systems support all time zone names. If the previous example does not work, MySQL might not be configured with time zone support. Contact your system administrator or refer to http://dev.mysql.com/doc/refman/5.0/en/ time-zone-support.html.

Formatting a Date

To display a date in a different format, use the DATE_FORMAT() function. The first argument is a date; the second argument is a format string, specified using a series of characters prefixed with a % sign. Other characters in the format string are included in the result verbatim.

The following example formats a date using the full textual day and
month names, and an ordinal suffix on the date:

```
mysql> SELECT DATE_FORMAT(NOW(), 'The date is %W %D %M %Y');
+----------------------------------------------+
| DATE_FORMAT(NOW(), 'The date is %W %D %M %Y') |
+----------------------------------------------+
| The date is Friday 28th October 2005          |
+----------------------------------------------+
1 row in set (0.00 sec)
```

Table 8.2 shows the full list of format characters for a date.

TABLE 8.2   Date Format Characters Used by DATE_FORMAT()

Character	Meaning
%a	Abbreviated weekday name (Sun–Sat)
%b	Abbreviated month name (Jan–Dec)
%c	Month number, no leading zero (1–12)
%D	Day of the month with ordinal suffix (1st–31st)
%d	Day of the month (1–31)
%j	Day of the year, three digits (001–366)
%M	Month name (January–December)
%m	Month number, two digits (01–12)
%U	Week number using Sunday as first day of week (01–53)
%u	Week number using Monday as first day of week (01–53)
%W	Weekday name (Sunday–Saturday)
%Y	Year, four digits
%y	Year, two digits

To format a date, you can still use DATE_FORMAT() with a different set of format codes. The following example shows just one way to format the current time returned by NOW():

```
mysql> SELECT DATE_FORMAT(NOW(), 'The time is %h:%i:%s %p');
+------------------------------------------------+
| DATE_FORMAT(NOW(), 'The time is %h:%i:%s %p') |
+------------------------------------------------+
| The time is 04:19:36 PM                        |
+------------------------------------------------+
1 row in set (0.00 sec)
```

Table 8.3 lists all the format characters that can be used to format a time.

TABLE 8.3   Time Format Characters Used by DATE_FORMAT()

Character	Meaning
%H	Hour on 24-hour clock, two digits (00–23)
%h	Hour on 12-hour clock (01–12)
%i	Minutes, two digits (01–59)
%l	Hour on 12-hour clock, no leading zero (1–12)
%p	A.M. or P.M.
%r	Time on 12-hour clock as HH:MM:SS
%s	Seconds, two digits (00–59)
%T	Time on 24-hour clock as HH:MM:SS

Percent   To include a literal percent character in a date format string, use %%.

Extracting Part of a Date

You can use the EXTRACT() function to return part of the date. Similar behavior can be achieved using DATE_FORMAT(), but whereas that function returns a formatted string, EXTRACT() returns a numeric result.

The syntax of EXTRACT() uses the same interval specifier as date arithmetic, with the keyword FROM. The following example returns the day number part of the current date:

```
mysql> SELECT EXTRACT(DAY FROM NOW());
+-------------------------+
| EXTRACT(DAY FROM NOW()) |
+-------------------------+
|                      28 |
+-------------------------+
1 row in set (0.01 sec)
```

If you use a compound unit, the values are returned as a single number with the most significant value first. The following example returns the year and month from the current date:

```
mysql> SELECT EXTRACT(YEAR_MONTH FROM NOW());
+--------------------------------+
| EXTRACT(YEAR_MONTH FROM NOW()) |
+--------------------------------+
|                         200510 |
+--------------------------------+
1 row in set (0.00 sec)
```

Date Arithmetic

To compute the difference between two dates, use the DATEDIFF() function. Given two date arguments, DATEDIFF() returns the number of days between the second date and the first.

```
mysql> SELECT DATEDIFF('2006-01-20', '2005-11-10');
+--------------------------------------+
| DATEDIFF('2006-01-20', '2005-11-10') |
+--------------------------------------+
|                                   71 |
+--------------------------------------+
1 row in set (0.00 sec)
```

If the second date is greater than the first, the value returned is negative, as shown in this example:

```
mysql> SELECT DATEDIFF('2005-12-31', '2006-01-01');
+--------------------------------------+
| DATEDIFF('2005-12-31', '2006-01-01') |
+--------------------------------------+
|                                   -1 |
+--------------------------------------+
1 row in set (0.00 sec)
```

 Time Components   If you run DATEDIFF() on two date values that include a time component, the time elements are simply ignored in the calculation. The calculation is performed on the dates only.

You can use TIMEDIFF() to calculate the difference between two times. The result returned is a time value, as shown in the following example:

```
mysql> SELECT TIMEDIFF('12:00', '10:30');
+----------------------------+
| TIMEDIFF('12:00', '10:30') |
+----------------------------+
| 01:30:00                   |
+----------------------------+
1 row in set (0.02 sec)
```

The arguments to TIMEDIFF() contain date elements, but a time value is still returned—there is not a date component in the result. The following example shows that when the times are more than a day apart, the time value returned is larger than 24 hours:

```
mysql> SELECT TIMEDIFF('2006-01-31 12:00', '2006-01-30 09:30');
+--------------------------------------------------+
| TIMEDIFF('2006-01-31 12:00', '2006-01-30 09:30') |
+--------------------------------------------------+
| 26:30:00                                         |
+--------------------------------------------------+
1 row in set (0.00 sec)
```

UNIX Time Stamps

UNIX time stamp format is a common way of representing time values as an integer. The numeric value is the number of seconds since midnight on January 1, 1970. The current time stamp value is a 10-digit number.

The UNIX_TIMESTAMP() function returns the time stamp value of a date. If it is called with no arguments, it returns the current time stamp.

```
mysql> SELECT UNIX_TIMESTAMP('2006-01-01 12:45:31');
+---------------------------------------+
| UNIX_TIMESTAMP('2006-01-01 12:45:31') |
+---------------------------------------+
|                            1136119531 |
+---------------------------------------+
1 row in set (0.00 sec)
```

To convert a time stamp to a MySQL date, use FROM_UNIXTIME().

```
mysql> SELECT FROM_UNIXTIME(1136119531);
+---------------------------+
| FROM_UNIXTIME(1136119531) |
+---------------------------+
| 2006-01-01 12:45:31       |
+---------------------------+
1 row in set (0.00 sec)
```

Summary

In this lesson, you learned how to work with date and time values in MySQL. In the next lesson, you will learn how to use aggregating functions to produce summary information.

LESSON 9

Summarizing Data

In this lesson, you learn how to use MySQL's aggregate functions to produce summary information in a query.

Aggregate Functions

MySQL provides five aggregate functions that enable you to summarize table data without retrieving every row. By using these functions, you can find the total number of rows in a dataset, the sum of the values, or the highest, lowest, and average values.

The COUNT() Function

The COUNT() function counts values in a query. You can perform a count on a single column by putting the column name in parentheses. More commonly, though, you use COUNT(*) to return the total number of rows returned by a query.

The following example counts the total number of orders that have been placed in the sample database:

```
mysql> SELECT COUNT(*)
    -> FROM orders;
+----------+
| COUNT(*) |
+----------+
|        7 |
+----------+
1 row in set (0.00 sec)
```

NULL **Values**   When COUNT() is called with a column name, it counts only the number of rows that have a value in that column. If the data in that column is NULL, it is not counted.

To find the number of unique values in a column, use COUNT() with the DISTINCT keyword. The following example finds the total number of customer contacts in the database and also the number of unique last names:

```
mysql> SELECT COUNT(*), COUNT(DISTINCT last_name)
    -> FROM customer_contacts;
+----------+---------------------------+
| COUNT(*) | COUNT(DISTINCT last_name) |
+----------+---------------------------+
|       11 |                        10 |
+----------+---------------------------+
1 row in set (0.02 sec)
```

The SUM() Function

The SUM() function computes a total from the data in a specified column. For example, you can use the following query to return the total number of units ordered of a particular product:

```
mysql> SELECT SUM(quantity)
    -> FROM order_lines
    -> WHERE product_code = 'MAXI';
+---------------+
| SUM(quantity) |
+---------------+
|            48 |
+---------------+
1 row in set (0.00 sec)
```

If you include an expression within SUM(), it is evaluated for each row of data and the total result is returned, as shown in the following query:

```
mysql> SELECT SUM(quantity + 1)
    -> FROM order_lines
    -> WHERE product_code = 'MAXI';
```

```
+-------------------+
| SUM(quantity + 1) |
+-------------------+
|                54 |
+-------------------+
1 row in set (0.00 sec)
```

You can use SUM() with a conditional expression to return the number of rows that meet the condition. Because the expression evaluates to 1 each time the condition is true and 0 each time it is false, the following query finds the number of products that weigh less than 5 pounds:

```
mysql> SELECT SUM(weight < 5)
    -> FROM products;
+-----------------+
| SUM(weight < 5) |
+-----------------+
|               2 |
+-----------------+
1 row in set (0.00 sec)
```

The AVG() Function

You can use the AVG() function to compute an average of the data in a specified column. The following query returns the average weight of all the items in the products table:

```
mysql> SELECT AVG(weight)
    -> FROM products;
+-------------+
| AVG(weight) |
+-------------+
|    4.666667 |
+-------------+
1 row in set (0.00 sec)
```

The AVG() function computes a *mean* average. The same result could be performed using SUM() and COUNT(), as follows:

```
mysql> SELECT SUM(weight) / COUNT(weight)
    -> FROM products;
+----------------------------+
| SUM(weight) / COUNT(weight) |
+----------------------------+
|                     4.6667 |
+----------------------------+
1 row in set (0.00 sec)
```

 NULL Values   NULL values are excluded when computing an average with AVG().

The MIN() and MAX() Functions

The MIN() and MAX() functions return the smallest and greatest values from a column, respectively. The following query finds the least expensive product in the database:

```
mysql> SELECT MIN(price)
    -> FROM products;
+------------+
| MIN(price) |
+------------+
|       5.99 |
+------------+
1 row in set (0.00 sec)
```

The next query finds the date of the most recent order placed by using MAX() on the date_ordered column of the orders table.

```
mysql> SELECT MAX(order_date)
    -> FROM orders;
+-----------------+
| MAX(order_date) |
+-----------------+
| 2006-02-05      |
+-----------------+
1 row in set (0.01 sec)
```

Grouping Data

Grouping is a SQL feature that enables you to produce summary data on groups of rows in the result set.

Consider the first example in this lesson, in which you performed a query using COUNT(*) to find the total number of orders in the database. Suppose that now you want to know the total number of orders for each customer.

By adding a WHERE clause, you could restrict the count using a customer_code value, but you would have to perform this query once for each customer to find all the totals. By grouping data instead, you can perform the aggregate function for each customer in a single query.

The GROUP BY Clause

To tell MySQL how to group the data in a query, you add a GROUP BY clause. This must appear after the WHERE clause and before any ORDER BY. As with the ORDER BY clause, the GROUP BY keywords are followed by one or a list of column names.

The GROUP BY clause collates rows in which the column specified contains the same value so that many table rows are returned as a single row of data. With data grouped in this way, you can add an aggregate function to the SELECT statement, and that function will be evaluated for each table row that was included in the group.

The following query finds the total number of orders for each customer in the database:

```
mysql> SELECT customer_code, COUNT(*)
    -> FROM orders
    -> GROUP BY customer_code;
+---------------+----------+
| customer_code | COUNT(*) |
+---------------+----------+
| MUSGRP        |        2 |
| PRESINC       |        2 |
| SCICORP       |        3 |
+---------------+----------+
3 rows in set (0.02 sec)
```

Grouping Without an aggregate function, the GROUP BY clause simply causes MySQL to return only unique rows—just like the DISTINCT keyword.

Using Column Aliases

When you want to group data on a calculated column, use a column alias to give the column a manageable name. You can give the column alias in the GROUP BY clause.

The following example selects the number of orders in the database grouped by month, using the DATE_FORMAT() function to return only the month and year from the order_date column:

```
mysql> SELECT DATE_FORMAT(order_date, '%M %Y') AS order_month,
    ->        COUNT(*)
    -> FROM orders
    -> GROUP BY order_month
    -> ORDER BY order_date;
+---------------+----------+
| order_month   | COUNT(*) |
+---------------+----------+
| January 2006  |        3 |
| February 2006 |        4 |
+---------------+----------+
2 rows in set (0.00 sec)
```

Although you could specify the full column calculation in the GROUP BY clause, it's clearly more convenient to use a table alias here.

Note that the ORDER BY clause in this query uses order_date, not order_month—you want the results to be shown in date order, not alphabetically, which would show February before January.

Ordering If you do not supply an ORDER BY clause, the query will be ordered on the columns specified in the GROUP BY clause. If you want, you can also use the column alias in the ORDER BY clause.

Grouping on Several Columns

It's possible to group by more than one column by specifying a comma-separated list of column names in the GROUP BY clause. When you do this, grouping requires that all columns specified contain the same value.

The following example groups data from the orders table by both month and customer. The summary data produced shows a breakdown of the number of orders placed by each customer in each month.

```
mysql> SELECT DATE_FORMAT(order_date, '%M %Y') AS order_month,
    ->          customer_code,
    ->          COUNT(*)
    -> FROM orders
    -> GROUP BY order_month, customer_code
    -> ORDER BY order_date;
+---------------+---------------+----------+
| order_month   | customer_code | COUNT(*) |
+---------------+---------------+----------+
| January 2006  | PRESINC       |        2 |
| January 2006  | SCICORP       |        1 |
| February 2006 | MUSGRP        |        2 |
| February 2006 | SCICORP       |        2 |
+---------------+---------------+----------+
4 rows in set (0.00 sec)
```

The order in which the columns are given in the GROUP BY clause does not affect the grouping. The following example reversed the column order so that customers appear first, followed by a breakdown of their orders by month. Although it would make for more readable code to specify the grouped columns in the same order they are selected, this example shows that it does not actually affect the query results:

```
mysql> SELECT customer_code,
    ->          DATE_FORMAT(order_date, '%M %Y') AS order_month,
    ->          COUNT(*)
    -> FROM orders
    -> GROUP BY order_month, customer_code
    -> ORDER BY customer_code;
+---------------+---------------+----------+
| customer_code | order_month   | COUNT(*) |
+---------------+---------------+----------+
| MUSGRP        | February 2006 |        2 |
| PRESINC       | January 2006  |        2 |
```

```
| SCICORP        | January 2006   |        1 |
| SCICORP        | February 2006  |        2 |
+---------------+---------------+---------+
4 rows in set (0.00 sec)
```

Filtering Summary Data

In Lesson 4, "Filtering and Sorting Data," you learned how to filter data using a WHERE clause and a condition that references a table column. You cannot reference a column produced by an aggregate function in a WHERE clause. Instead, you must use HAVING.

The HAVING Clause

The HAVING clause must appear after the GROUP BY clause. It contains a conditional expression that can reference the result of an aggregate function in the query.

The following query finds dates on which more than one order was placed. It groups data from the orders table by order_date and uses a HAVING clause on the COUNT(*) aggregate to find where that group is made up of more than one table row.

```
mysql> SELECT order_date, COUNT(*)
    -> FROM orders
    -> GROUP BY order_date
    -> HAVING COUNT(*) > 1;
+------------+----------+
| order_date | COUNT(*) |
+------------+----------+
| 2006-01-23 |        2 |
| 2006-02-02 |        2 |
+------------+----------+
2 rows in set (0.01 sec)
```

Similarly, the next example looks at the order_items table and finds which products have shipped at least 30 units. In this example, a column alias is used on the summary column and also in the HAVING clause.

```
mysql> SELECT product_code, SUM(quantity) as num_shipped
    -> FROM order_lines
    -> GROUP BY product_code
    -> HAVING num_shipped > 30;
+--------------+-------------+
| product_code | num_shipped |
+--------------+-------------+
| MAXI         |          48 |
| MINI         |          36 |
+--------------+-------------+
2 rows in set (0.00 sec)
```

Summary

In this lesson, you learned how to produce summary information using MySQL's aggregate functions and how to group data using the GROUP BY clause. In the next part of this book, you will learn how to construct more complex SQL queries.

LESSON 10

Using Subqueries

In this lesson, you learn how queries can be nested in MySQL so that the result of one query can determine the result of another query.

Understanding Subqueries

A subquery is a query that is embedded within another query. Subqueries are sometimes also referred to as *subselects* because one SELECT statement appears within another. Let's look at how subqueries can be useful.

Filtering by Subquery

You can use the result of a query like you use a list of values with the IN operator to filter a query based on the result of another query. The subquery appears in parentheses after the IN keyword.

The following query fetches all columns from the products table, but only for those product codes that were part of order number 1:

```
mysql> SELECT *
    -> FROM products
    -> WHERE product_code IN (
    ->   SELECT product_code
    ->   FROM order_lines
    ->   WHERE order_id = 1
    -> );
+--------------+---------------+--------+-------+
| product_code | name          | weight | price |
+--------------+---------------+--------+-------+
| MINI         | Small product |   1.50 |  5.99 |
| MAXI         | Large product |   8.00 | 15.99 |
+--------------+---------------+--------+-------+
2 rows in set (0.00 sec)
```

Formatting Subqueries In the previous example, the subquery was indented from the main query for clarity. Remember, you can use as many spaces and carriage returns as you like to keep things readable.

Let's break down how MySQL evaluates this query. First, the subquery is executed to find a list of product codes. If you run the subquery on its own, you will see the following result:

```
mysql> SELECT product_code
    -> FROM order_lines
    -> WHERE order_id = 1;
+--------------+
| product_code |
+--------------+
| MINI         |
| MAXI         |
+--------------+
2 rows in set (0.00 sec)
```

So using this result, after evaluating the subquery, MySQL runs a query that is the same as the following:

```
mysql> SELECT *
    -> FROM products
    -> WHERE product_code IN ('MINI', 'MAXI');
+--------------+---------------+--------+-------+
| product_code | name          | weight | price |
+--------------+---------------+--------+-------+
| MINI         | Small product |   1.50 |  5.99 |
| MAXI         | Large product |   8.00 | 15.99 |
+--------------+---------------+--------+-------+
2 rows in set (0.01 sec)
```

As you can see, using a subquery in this type of situation saves you from having to perform two queries separately and insert the result of the first into the second—either yourself by hand or using a data structure in a programming language.

Query Performance   The syntax of a subquery makes your SQL statement very easy to read, but often there are more efficient ways of performing the same task. You will learn how to perform similar operations using table joins in the next lesson.

The Correlated Subquery

If a subquery involves a table that also appears in the outer SELECT statement, it is known as a correlated subquery.

MySQL cannot evaluate this type of subquery by feeding the result of the inner SELECT statement into the outer query because each SELECT statement relies on values from the other.

To reference the same table more than once in the same query, you must use table aliases. These work just the same as the column aliases you have already come across, but they enable you to qualify columns from a table using an abbreviated alias.

To alias a table, give it an alias name immediately after the table name in the FROM clause. The AS keyword is optional for table aliases.

The following example uses a correlated subquery on the order_lines table, comparing the average quantity of each product ordered at a time to every order that included that product in turn. The result is a list of orders in which a higher than average quantity of each product was shipped.

```
mysql> SELECT order_id, product_code, quantity
    -> FROM order_lines ol1
    -> WHERE quantity > (
    ->   SELECT AVG(quantity)
    ->   FROM order_lines ol2
    ->   WHERE ol2.product_code = ol1.product_code
    -> );
+----------+--------------+----------+
| order_id | product_code | quantity |
+----------+--------------+----------+
|        2 | MAXI         |       12 |
```

```
|         3 | MINI          |        16 |
|         4 | MINI          |        16 |
|         4 | MAXI          |        10 |
|         5 | MAXI          |        10 |
+-----------+---------------+-----------+
5 rows in set (0.00 sec)
```

The query fetches data from the `order_lines` table twice, aliased to `ol1` and `ol2`. The `tablename.column` notation is used to qualify a column name in SQL; in this case, however, the table name would be the same, so two different aliases are required.

This example is a correlated subquery because the inner subquery cannot be executed outside this complete SQL statement. It references `ol1.product_code`, a column from the outer query.

Correlated Subquery Performance Although it is a powerful SQL construct, the correlated subquery can be slow to execute if the result sets from each SELECT statement are large. If there is another way to find the same information in SQL, it will probably run faster than a correlated subquery.

Subquerying the Same Table

The following example uses a subquery on the same table as the outer query. Its purpose is to find records from the `customer_contacts` table that share attributes with a known record, but one in which the key value you actually want to search on is not known.

```
mysql> SELECT first_name, last_name
    -> FROM customer_contacts
    -> WHERE customer_code = (
    ->     SELECT customer_code
    ->     FROM customer_contacts
    ->     WHERE first_name = 'Benjamin'
    ->     AND last_name = 'Franklin'
    -> );
```

```
+-------------+------------+
| first_name  | last_name  |
+-------------+------------+
| Albert      | Einstein   |
| Charles     | Darwin     |
| Marie       | Curie      |
| Benjamin    | Franklin   |
+-------------+------------+
4 rows in set (0.00 sec)
```

Note that this is not a correlated subquery. The subquery can be evaluated independently of the outer query and the result used as the argument to the = operator. The result is all the contacts who are related to the same customer record as the given contact name.

Using the equals operator with a subquery means you must be sure that the subquery returns only one row; otherwise, you must use IN. With the sample database, you know there is only one Benjamin Franklin, so there is no problem. However, be aware that MySQL generates an error as shown here if the subquery returns more than one row for an equals operator:

```
mysql> SELECT first_name, last_name
    -> FROM customer_contacts
    -> WHERE customer_code = (
    ->     SELECT customer_code
    ->     FROM customer_contacts
    ->     WHERE first_name = 'Benjamin'
    -> );
ERROR 1242 (21000): Subquery returns more than 1 row
```

Using Subqueries as Calculated Fields

You can actually nest a query in the column list section of a SELECT statement. The query executes the subquery and returns its value as a column in the result set for each row in the main query.

The following example retrieves each product from the database along with a subquery column that finds the total quantity ordered for each product in turn:

```
mysql> SELECT p.name,
    ->      (SELECT SUM(ol.quantity)
    ->      FROM order_lines ol
    ->      WHERE ol.product_code = p.product_code) AS subquery
    -> FROM products p;
+-----------------+----------+
| name            | subquery |
+-----------------+----------+
| Small product   |       36 |
| Medium product  |       10 |
| Large product   |       48 |
+-----------------+----------+
3 rows in set (0.00 sec)
```

 Table Joins   This subquery example involves a type of table join in which the filter on the query involves a column value from another table. Joins are covered in more detail in the next lesson.

Using Subqueries as Tables

In the same way that the result of a subquery can be used with an operator in the WHERE clause, you can use a subquery as a table in the FROM clause.

This feature will become more useful when you have learned how to perform advanced table joins in the next few chapters. For now, you'll see how it works with a trivial example.

The following query uses a subquery in place of a table in the FROM clause. The subquery returns a subset of the data from the customer_contacts table.

Performing a SELECT * on that virtual table can return only the columns included in the subquery. The WHERE clause in the main query takes effect after the data has already been filtered in the subquery.

```
mysql> SELECT *
    -> FROM (
    ->    SELECT first_name, last_name
    ->    FROM customer_contacts
    ->    WHERE customer_code = 'SCICORP'
    -> ) scicorp_customers
    -> WHERE first_name = 'Benjamin';
+------------+-----------+
| first_name | last_name |
+------------+-----------+
| Benjamin   | Franklin  |
+------------+-----------+
1 row in set (0.00 sec)
```

When using a subquery as a table, you must give the subquery a table alias or MySQL will return an error. In the previous example, the virtual table was aliased to scicorp_customers.

Summary

In this lesson, you learned about the ways in which subqueries can be used in MySQL. In the next lesson, you will learn how tables in a relational database are joined in a SQL query.

LESSON 11
Joining Tables

In this lesson, you learn what joins are and how they are used in SELECT statements to retrieve data from different tables.

Understanding Joins

The capability to join tables is probably the most important feature of MySQL, so it is important that you understand how to construct a SELECT statement that includes a join.

Understanding Relational Tables

MySQL is a relational database. This means that data records can be split across several tables in a logical way. You will learn how to design a relational database in Lesson 16, "Designing Your Database," so for now, you'll consider a simple example from the sample tables that you have already seen.

A relationship exists between the customers and customer_contacts tables. There might be more than one contact person for each customer, assuming that a customer is a company and that you can deal with people in different departments. By splitting this information into two tables, you avoid duplicating data that is always the same for contacts within the same company.

Duplicate Data   By not duplicating columns, you not only reduce the amount of storage required for the database, but you also eliminate the possibility of data inconsistency that might otherwise exist. For instance, when a company's details are stored in just one record in the customers table instead of in every row in the customer_contacts table, there is no danger that the customer data will be inconsistent from one record to another.

To keep the examples in this book simple, the sample tables contain a much smaller amount of information than you would find in a real-world database. Still, the concept is the same. The sample table customers contains a name field, which is the name of the customer. In a live database, this table would also contain a corporate address and any other information that is the same for a customer—and is the same for all the contact persons for that customer.

The customer_contacts table is used to store multiple contacts for a customer. The customer_code field in this table acts as a link back to the customer data. The value of contacts.customer_code corresponds to the customers.customer_code value and is the *key* field used when joining these tables.

Keys   The customer_code column in customers is a *primary key* field. It contains a unique value that can be used to identify exactly one record from the table. The column with the same name in customer_contacts is known as a *foreign key*. You will learn more about keys in Lesson 17, "Keys and Indexes."

Joining Two Tables

To join two tables, give both their names in the FROM clause of a SELECT statement. To indicate the relationship between the two tables, you must include an appropriate condition in the WHERE clause.

The following query joins the customers and customer_contacts tables to produce the complete contact information from the sample database. Because this query retrieves the entire contacts database, there is only one WHERE condition; this tells MySQL that the relationship between the tables is that the customer_code value is a reference to the customer_code column in customers.

```
mysql> SELECT name,
    -> CONCAT(last_name, ', ', first_name) as contact_name
    -> FROM customers, customer_contacts
    -> WHERE customers.customer_code =
    ->       customer_contacts.customer_code
    -> ORDER BY name, contact_name;
+------------------------+----------------------+
| name                   | contact_name         |
+------------------------+----------------------+
| Musicians of America   | Britten, Benjamin    |
| Musicians of America   | Gershwin, George     |
| Musicians of America   | Lennon, John         |
| Presidents Incorporated | Lincoln, Abraham    |
| Presidents Incorporated | Nixon, Richard      |
| Presidents Incorporated | Roosevelt, Franklin |
| Presidents Incorporated | Roosevelt, Theodore |
| Science Corporation    | Curie, Marie         |
| Science Corporation    | Darwin, Charles      |
| Science Corporation    | Einstein, Albert     |
| Science Corporation    | Franklin, Benjamin   |
+------------------------+----------------------+
11 rows in set (0.02 sec)
```

Column Naming   The sample tables in this book have

used a naming convention in which each foreign key has the same name as the corresponding primary key in the other table.

However, this is not a requirement. Another popular convention is to name the primary key in each table as simply id or code. For example, the customer_code value in customer_contacts would relate to a column named code in customers.

Cartesian Products

The condition in the WHERE clause that indicates the relationship between joined tables is very important. To see why, look at what happens when you specify two tables in the FROM clause without any conditions.

Two small tables are included in the sample database, named t1 and t2. These tables contain just a few rows to demonstrate joins. First, familiarize yourself with their data:

```
mysql> SELECT * FROM t1;
+----+--------+
| id | letter |
+----+--------+
|  1 | A      |
|  2 | B      |
|  3 | C      |
+----+--------+
3 rows in set (0.01 sec)

mysql> SELECT * FROM t2;
+----+--------+
| id | letter |
+----+--------+
|  1 | X      |
|  2 | Y      |
|  3 | Z      |
+----+--------+
3 rows in set (0.00 sec)
```

Now perform a join on the two tables, with no condition specified.

```
mysql> SELECT *
    -> FROM t1, t2;
+----+--------+----+--------+
| id | letter | id | letter |
+----+--------+----+--------+
|  1 | A      |  1 | X      |
|  2 | B      |  1 | X      |
|  3 | C      |  1 | X      |
|  1 | A      |  2 | Y      |
|  2 | B      |  2 | Y      |
|  3 | C      |  2 | Y      |
|  1 | A      |  3 | Z      |
|  2 | B      |  3 | Z      |
|  3 | C      |  3 | Z      |
+----+--------+----+--------+
9 rows in set (0.00 sec)
```

As you can see, each row from t1 is combined with each row from t2. Three rows in each table produce a join, resulting in a total of nine pairs of records. This is known as a *Cartesian product*, and it is rarely the result you would want from a query.

SELECT * Notice how the SELECT * notation in the previous example caused every column from both tables to be returned. As a result, two columns named id and two named letter were returned. These columns belong to the tables in the order given in the FROM clause.

The total number of rows returned is the product of the number of rows in each table. You can imagine how large the resulting data set can grow when the individual tables contain a large number of rows themselves.

Cross Joins A Cartesian product is sometimes known as a *cross join*.

Adding a WHERE condition to this join instructs MySQL to filter out the pairs of records for which there is no relationship between the data. This is the majority of the rows that would be returned in a Cartesian product. Assuming a relationship between the id column in each table, the join then produces the following result:

```
mysql> SELECT *
    -> FROM t1, t2
    -> WHERE t1.id = t2.id;
+----+--------+----+--------+
| id | letter | id | letter |
+----+--------+----+--------+
|  1 | A      |  1 | X      |
|  2 | B      |  2 | Y      |
|  3 | C      |  3 | Z      |
+----+--------+----+--------+
3 rows in set (0.00 sec)
```

Take a moment to look back at the result of the Cartesian product, and you will see that the three rows returned by the previous example appear, but the other rows have been discarded.

Join Types   A join that involves a condition in which columns in two tables are specified as equal is known as an *equijoin* or *inner join*. You will learn about other types of joins in Lesson 12, "Creating Advanced Joins."

Foreign Keys   Even if your table definition has a foreign key defined (you will learn how to do this in Lesson 17), you must include a WHERE clause that specifies the join condition. The relationship to be used for a join is never stored at the database level.

Joining Multiple Tables

You can join more than two tables in one query by specifying all the table names in the FROM clause. The following example uses the relationships among orders, order_lines, and products tables to produce an order history for a particular customer:

```
mysql> SELECT o.order_id, o.order_date, l.quantity, p.name
    -> FROM orders o, order_lines l, products p
    -> WHERE o.order_id = l.order_id
    -> AND p.product_code = l.product_code
    -> AND o.customer_code = 'SCICORP'
    -> ORDER BY o.order_date;
+----------+------------+----------+----------------+
| order_id | order_date | quantity | name           |
+----------+------------+----------+----------------+
|        3 | 2006-01-23 |       16 | Small product  |
|        4 | 2006-02-02 |       16 | Small product  |
|        4 | 2006-02-02 |       10 | Large product  |
|        5 | 2006-02-05 |       10 | Medium product |
|        5 | 2006-02-05 |       10 | Large product  |
+----------+------------+----------+----------------+
5 rows in set (0.00 sec)
```

To perform an equijoin on multiple tables, a condition in the WHERE clause must specify a relationship from every table to another table. In this example, there are relationships between orders and order_lines, and between order_lines and products.

Each row in order_lines adds the specified quantity of a product to an order. The order_id column in order_lines joins that table to orders, and the product_code column joins it to products. The first two conditions in the WHERE clause indicate these relationships. The third filter is used to return only the order history for SCICORP.

Joining Tables   In the previous example, because there is no direct relationship between orders and products, no condition in the WHERE clause tries to link these tables.

Although each table joined should have a relationship to another table in the query, every table does not have to be—and usually will not be—related to *every* other table.

Summary

In this lesson, you learned how to perform a join on two or more tables based on a relationship between the primary key and foreign key columns. In the next lesson, you will learn about other types of joins that can be performed in MySQL.

LESSON 12

Creating Advanced Joins

In this lesson, you learn how to perform different types of joins on MySQL tables using the JOIN keyword.

The JOIN Keyword

In the previous lesson, you learned how to join two or more database tables by specifying a list of table names in the FROM clause of the SQL statement.

MySQL provides an alternate syntax using the JOIN keyword that allows several different types of table joins to be performed.

Inner Joins

An inner join, or equijoin, is a join that uses a condition to specify a relationship between tables in which a column in one table is equal to another column in the other table. In the previous lesson, you learned how to do this using the WHERE clause.

The alternative syntax uses the keyword phrase INNER JOIN to specify a table to join to and the keyword ON to specify a conditional clause that indicates the relationship between the tables.

The following example reproduces the query from Lesson 11, "Joining Tables," to retrieve all the customer contact information:

```
mysql> SELECT name,
    -> CONCAT(last_name, ', ', first_name) as contact_name
    -> FROM customers
```

```
    -> INNER JOIN customer_contacts
    -> ON customers.customer_code =
    ->       customer_contacts.customer_code
    -> ORDER BY name, contact_name;
+------------------------+---------------------+
| name                   | contact_name        |
+------------------------+---------------------+
| Musicians of America   | Britten, Benjamin   |
| Musicians of America   | Gershwin, George    |
| Musicians of America   | Lennon, John        |
| Presidents Incorporated | Lincoln, Abraham    |
| Presidents Incorporated | Nixon, Richard      |
| Presidents Incorporated | Roosevelt, Franklin |
| Presidents Incorporated | Roosevelt, Theodore |
| Science Corporation    | Curie, Marie        |
| Science Corporation    | Darwin, Charles     |
| Science Corporation    | Einstein, Albert    |
| Science Corporation    | Franklin, Benjamin  |
+------------------------+---------------------+
11 rows in set (0.00 sec)
```

The keywords INNER JOIN appear immediately after the FROM clause and before any filtering is specified. When you use JOIN, the relationship between tables is defined after using the ON keyword instead of WHERE. This syntax for a join is longer, but often it is more readable because the WHERE clause is used only to filter the resulting data set.

Check back to the corresponding example in the previous lesson, and you will see that its WHERE clause is identical to the ON clause given previously.

 Using JOIN Whether you put multiple tables in the FROM clause and specify the join condition in the WHERE clause, or use JOIN ... ON is a matter of preference. Use whichever format you feel most comfortable with.

Joining Multiple Tables

To join multiple tables using the JOIN ... ON syntax, each table has its own JOIN keyword and its own ON clause immediately afterward.

The following example reproduces the query from Lesson 11 that
retrieves the order history for a given customer, joining the orders,
order_lines, and products tables:

```
mysql> SELECT o.order_id, o.order_date, l.quantity, p.name
    -> FROM orders o
    -> INNER JOIN order_lines l
    -> ON o.order_id = l.order_id
    -> INNER JOIN products p
    -> ON p.product_code = l.product_code
    -> WHERE o.customer_code = 'SCICORP'
    -> ORDER BY o.order_date;
+----------+------------+----------+----------------+
| order_id | order_date | quantity | name           |
+----------+------------+----------+----------------+
|        3 | 2006-01-23 |       16 | Small product  |
|        4 | 2006-02-02 |       16 | Small product  |
|        4 | 2006-02-02 |       10 | Large product  |
|        5 | 2006-02-05 |       10 | Medium product |
|        5 | 2006-02-05 |       10 | Large product  |
+----------+------------+----------+----------------+
5 rows in set (0.00 sec)
```

In this example, the orders table appears in the FROM clause, and
order_lines and products are each given after an INNER JOIN keyword.
This is the logical order in which to write the query because it has a hier-
archical structure—orders contain order lines, which, in turn, reference
products. The orders table is referenced in the WHERE clause.

However, when using INNER JOIN, the tables can be specified in any
order without affecting the outcome of the query.

 Inner Joins   The majority of joins you will want to
perform are inner joins, so this is the default behavior
for the JOIN keyword. You can use JOIN on its own
instead of INNER JOIN, and your query will work the
same way.

The ON Clause   The ON clause works just like a WHERE clause but is specific to a join condition. If you need to, you can add extra conditions to the ON clause using AND, just as you can with WHERE.

Cross Joins

You saw in the previous lesson that if no relationship between joined tables is given in the WHERE clause, a Cartesian product or *cross join* is produced.

The ON keyword is not required to appear after the JOIN keyword, so the same result can be obtained using INNER JOIN and no ON clause.

However, for readability, you can use the CROSS JOIN keyword to show in your query that the Cartesian product is the desired result. The following example reproduces the cross join between sample tables t1 and t2 from the previous lesson:

```
mysql> SELECT *
    -> FROM t1
    -> CROSS JOIN t2;
+----+--------+----+--------+
| id | letter | id | letter |
+----+--------+----+--------+
|  1 | A      |  1 | X      |
|  2 | B      |  1 | X      |
|  3 | C      |  1 | X      |
|  1 | A      |  2 | Y      |
|  2 | B      |  2 | Y      |
|  3 | C      |  2 | Y      |
|  1 | A      |  3 | Z      |
|  2 | B      |  3 | Z      |
|  3 | C      |  3 | Z      |
+----+--------+----+--------+
9 rows in set (0.01 sec)
```

You will use a cross join very rarely, so it is helpful to use this syntax to make it clear that you actually want to perform this type of join.

Self-Joins

Sometimes you want to join a table to itself. You can do this either by putting the same table name in the FROM clause twice or by using that table after a JOIN keyword.

The following example uses a self-join to find people in the customer_ contacts table who belong to the same company as a named person. You achieved the same result in Lesson 10, "Using Subqueries," using a subquery—this is a different approach to the same problem.

```
mysql> SELECT c2.first_name, c2.last_name
    -> FROM customer_contacts c1
    -> JOIN customer_contacts c2
    -> ON c1.customer_code = c2.customer_code
    -> WHERE c1.first_name = 'Benjamin'
    -> AND c1.last_name = 'Franklin';
+------------+-----------+
| first_name | last_name |
+------------+-----------+
| Albert     | Einstein  |
| Charles    | Darwin    |
| Marie      | Curie     |
| Benjamin   | Franklin  |
+------------+-----------+
4 rows in set (0.00 sec)
```

In this example, the customer_contacts table is used twice, as an alias to c1 and c2. By joining the table to itself in the customer_code field, the result is a data set that includes a pair of records for every person alongside every other person in the company. The filter in the WHERE clause restricts the output of the query to only find those contacts who share a company with Charles Darwin.

Of course, if you already knew the customer code that corresponded to the person you were searching for, the query would need to look at customer_contacts only once and filter using the appropriate condition on customer_code. The self-join is necessary only because the known value—a contact person's name—cannot be used to perform the required filter directly.

Aliases with Self-Joins When you join a table to itself, it is vital that you give each table an alias. The tables will, of course, contain exactly the same columns, so you must use aliases to qualify the columns you want to reference.

Note that the columns selected in the previous example are from the table aliased to c2, not c1. The filter is performed on values in c1 and restricts the records returned to a particular name. Therefore, if you had selected the name values from c1, they would all be the same.

Self-Joins vs. Subqueries You have now seen two different ways to find the same information: using a self-join and a subquery. The "best" method often depends on the nature of the tables and the data involved.

In the very small sample database, you will not notice any difference in performance between the two methods. In a real-world system, however, if you find that one method is particularly slow, see if another approach to your query speeds things up.

Natural Joins

The keyword phrase NATURAL JOIN performs a join on two tables without needing an ON or WHERE clause to specify the relationship between the tables. Instead, MySQL assumes that the tables are related by all the columns that have the same name in both tables.

Whether you can use NATURAL JOIN depends on the column-naming convention used. For instance, in the sample database are columns named product_code in both the products and order_lines tables. The relationship between these tables is suitable for a NATURAL JOIN, as shown in the following example:

```
mysql> SELECT p.name, ol.quantity, p.price
    -> FROM order_lines ol
    -> NATURAL JOIN products p
    -> WHERE order_id = 1;
+---------------+----------+-------+
| name          | quantity | price |
+---------------+----------+-------+
| Small product |        4 |  5.99 |
| Large product |        2 | 15.99 |
+---------------+----------+-------+
2 rows in set (0.00 sec)
```

If the relationship between two tables relies upon a join that references columns that do not have the exact same name in both tables, you cannot use a NATURAL JOIN.

Outer Joins

Most joins return rows based on pairs of records from the two joined tables according to a given relationship. The outer join is different: All the rows from one table are returned, regardless of whether the relationship condition finds a matching row in the second table. When no corresponding record is found, columns that would otherwise contain values from the second table contain NULL.

Outer joins are useful in producing reports when you do not want to exclude a record from the result if it does not have any corresponding data in a joined table.

The following example uses an outer join to produce a report of the customer orders placed in the month of February only:

```
mysql> SELECT c.name, o.order_date
    -> FROM customers c
    -> LEFT OUTER JOIN orders o
    -> ON o.customer_code = c.customer_code
    -> AND o.order_date BETWEEN '2006-02-01' AND '2006-02-28';
+-------------------------+------------+
| name                    | order_date |
+-------------------------+------------+
| Presidents Incorporated | NULL       |
| Science Corporation     | 2006-02-02 |
| Science Corporation     | 2006-02-05 |
```

```
| Musicians of America   | 2006-02-01 |
| Musicians of America   | 2006-02-02 |
+------------------------+------------+
5 rows in set (0.00 sec)
```

Because Presidents Incorporated placed no orders in the date range specified—you will see in the orders table that orders were placed only in January—the order date returned is NULL.

> **LEFT JOIN**   The join keyword used in the previous example was LEFT OUTER JOIN, which is often shortened to LEFT JOIN. The LEFT keyword tells MySQL that the left table—the one specified first, in the FROM clause—should return every row with NULL in the right table when no match is found.
>
> You can use RIGHT OUTER JOIN or RIGHT JOIN to reverse the behavior so that the table given after JOIN must return every row.

Exactly one row is returned for a customer record when there is no corresponding order data, whereas the other customers have multiple rows returned according to their actual order history.

Notice that the filter on order_date is given in the ON clause, not the WHERE clause. Because the query returns a NULL order_date value for rows in customers that do have any orders, putting this filter in the WHERE clause would prevent those NULL values from being returned.

Summary

In this lesson, you learned how to perform inner joins, cross joins, natural joins, self-joins, and outer joins. In the next lesson, you will learn how to combine the result of two or more queries using set operations.

LESSON 13
Combining Queries

In this lesson, you learn how to combine the results from different queries using the UNION operator.

Understanding Combined Queries

Most SQL queries contain just one SELECT statement that can return data from one table, or several tables using a join. The technique of combining two or more independent queries into a single data set is usually known as a union or a compound query.

You might want to use this technique to retrieve records from two tables that have a similar structure in a single query. For instance, suppose you have archived off some data so that you have a customers table that contains your current customers and another table called old_customers.

These tables would have the same structure—or at least would share many common columns if new columns had been added to the customers table since the archive took place. Therefore, you could perform a query on this table that takes into account both current and archived customers. This would look something like the following:

```
SELECT name, telephone, email
FROM customers
UNION
SELECT name, telephone, email
FROM old_customers;
```

You can also use UNION to perform two different queries on the same table and combine the two results into a single data set.

The UNION Operator

The UNION operator is placed between two SQL queries to return a single result. A UNION is possible only if both queries return the same number of columns; otherwise, MySQL produces an error.

The following simple example demonstrates how the UNION operator works by combining two separate queries on the customer_contacts table:

```
mysql> SELECT first_name, last_name
    -> FROM customer_contacts
    -> WHERE customer_code = 'SCICORP'
    -> UNION
    -> SELECT first_name, last_name
    -> FROM customer_contacts
    -> WHERE customer_code = 'PRESINC';
+------------+-----------+
| first_name | last_name |
+------------+-----------+
| Albert     | Einstein  |
| Charles    | Darwin    |
| Marie      | Curie     |
| Benjamin   | Franklin  |
| Abraham    | Lincoln   |
| Richard    | Nixon     |
| Franklin   | Roosevelt |
| Theodore   | Roosevelt |
+------------+-----------+
8 rows in set (0.01 sec)
```

All the rows from the first query are returned first, followed by all the rows from the second query.

 Terminating Queries   When you execute a UNION using mysql, the terminating semicolon must only appear once, after the final query.

As you might have noticed, the previous example produced the same result that you can achieve using a single SELECT and an IN operator in the WHERE clause to select multiple values for customer_code.

The following example produces a result that cannot be accomplished any other way. Two different columns from the same table are selected in two different queries and combined using the UNION operator.

```
mysql> SELECT first_name
    -> FROM customer_contacts
    -> UNION
    -> SELECT last_name
    -> FROM customer_contacts;
+------------+
| first_name |
+------------+
| Abraham    |
| Richard    |
| Franklin   |
...
| Curie      |
| Gershwin   |
| Britten    |
| Lennon     |
+------------+
19 rows in set (0.00 sec)
```

The output is abbreviated to save space, but the full output contains every first_name and last_name value from the customer_contacts table, returned in a single column.

The UNION ALL Operator

Note that the total number of records returned by the previous query is 19. This might seem peculiar because you are selecting two values from each table row—you might expect the query to return an even number of values.

However, although the customer_contacts table contains 11 total rows, 3 of the values were duplicated; by default, the UNION operator returns only unique values. The duplicate names in this UNION are Benjamin (which appears as a first_name twice), Roosevelt (which appears as a last_name twice), and Franklin (which appears once as a first_name and once as a last_name).

If you want to ensure that every value in a UNION is returned, use the UNION ALL operator. This example would then look like the following:

```
mysql> SELECT first_name
    -> FROM customer_contacts
    -> UNION ALL
    -> SELECT last_name
    -> FROM customer_contacts;
+------------+
| first_name |
+------------+
| Abraham    |
| Richard    |
| Franklin   |
...
| Franklin   |
| Gershwin   |
| Britten    |
| Lennon     |
+------------+
22 rows in set (0.00 sec)
```

Sorting a UNION

Notice that in the previous example, the column heading is first_name, even though half the values returned were fetched from the last_name column. The column headings on UNION are taken from the column names or aliases in the first query only.

Therefore, to specify a sort order on a UNION, you must use the column name from the first query in the ORDER BY clause. The following is an example:

```
mysql> SELECT first_name
    -> FROM customer_contacts
    -> UNION
    -> SELECT last_name
    -> FROM customer_contacts
    -> ORDER BY first_name;
+------------+
| first_name |
+------------+
| Abraham    |
| Albert     |
| Benjamin   |
...
```

```
|  Richard    |
|  Roosevelt  |
|  Theodore   |
+-------------+
19 rows in set (0.02 sec)
```

It is important to realize that even though the ORDER BY clause appears to relate to the last query in the UNION, it actually applies to the entire result set. The individual SELECT statements are executed, then combined, and finally sorted using the ORDER BY rule.

 Ordering You cannot specify a sort order on individual queries in a UNION. MySQL will give an error if ORDER BY appears anywhere other than after the last SELECT statement.

Other Compound Operations

Some SQL-based databases include a wider range of operations that can be performed on two query result sets. These are MINUS or EXCEPT, in which the result contains only the rows from the first result that do not appear in the second, and INTERSECT, in which the result contains only rows that appear in both results.

MySQL does not understand these keywords, but there are ways to perform these operations using other techniques.

Performing a MINUS

The MINUS operator usually is placed between two queries. The result of the first query is returned, excluding any identical rows that are produced by the second query.

Using a similar example to the others in this chapter, you could use MINUS to find only first_name values from customer_contacts that are not also used as last_name values. The following query would return all the first_name values except for Franklin:

```
SELECT first_name
FROM customer_contacts
MINUS
SELECT last_name
FROM customer_contacts;
```

To reproduce this functionality in MySQL, you can rewrite the query as a subselect using the NOT IN operator, as follows:

```
SELECT first_name
FROM customer_contacts
WHERE first_name NOT IN (
  SELECT last_name
  FROM customer_contacts
);
```

An alternative, although not as readable, way to execute the same query uses a LEFT JOIN, as follows:

```
SELECT c1.first_name
FROM customer_contacts c1
LEFT JOIN customer_contacts c2
ON c1.first_name = c2.last_name
WHERE c2.last_name IS NULL;
```

Using a LEFT JOIN causes every row from c1 to be returned even if there is no matching row in c2. When there is no matching row, the values returned for c2 are all NULL. By filtering on the NULL values, you can exclude values for which the join was successful.

Optimizing MINUS   Both the techniques discussed in this section can produce very slow queries: The NOT IN operator cannot use an index, and a LEFT JOIN often has to process very large amounts of data in memory.

If neither performs well enough for your situation, consider using a temporary table instead, as discussed later in this lesson.

Performing an INTERSECT

The INTERSECT operator usually is placed between two queries; any data row that appears in the result of each individual query will appear in the overall result.

Using a similar example to the others in this chapter, you could use an INTERSECT to find only first_name values from customer_contacts that are also used as last_name values. The following query would find only the name Franklin from the sample tables:

```
SELECT first_name
FROM customer_contacts
INTERSECT
SELECT last_name
FROM customer_contacts;
```

An INTERSECT can be performed as a join in which you compare values from two different tables that are not otherwise related. For example, you could rewrite this query as follows:

```
SELECT c1.first_name
FROM customer_contacts c1
JOIN customer_contacts c2
ON c1.first_name = c2.last_name;
```

No relationship exists between first_name and last_name, but you can use these values as the join condition to simulate an INTERSECT.

Using Temporary Tables

Temporary tables in MySQL can be a powerful means of manipulating a data set. A temporary table exists only for the duration of your MySQL session, after which it is automatically deleted. Otherwise, it works just the same as a regular database table.

You will learn more about creating database tables in Lesson 14, "Creating and Modifying Tables." For now, consider some examples to simulate different types of a compound query.

Performing a UNION

To join two or more queries using a temporary table, you need to insert the data rows from both queries into the same table.

First, create a new table using the first query to define the columns. The result of this query will also be inserted into the table.

```
CREATE TEMPORARY TABLE myunion AS
SELECT first_name FROM customer_contacts;
```

In this case, a temporary table with a single column is created. You can then insert the result of the second query as follows:

```
INSERT INTO myunion
SELECT last_name FROM customer_contacts;
```

The table myunion now contains the union. In fact, if you performed a SELECT on this table, it would give the same result that a UNION ALL operation on the two queries would produce. To simulate a UNION, in which only distinct values are returned, execute this command:

```
SELECT DISTINCT first_name FROM myunion;
```

Performing a MINUS

To simulate a MINUS using a temporary table, first create a new table using the first query to define the columns and populate the initial data rows.

```
CREATE TEMPORARY TABLE myminus AS
SELECT first_name FROM customer_contacts;
```

Then delete the rows that also appear in the second query using a subquery, as follows:

```
DELETE FROM myminus
WHERE first_name IN (
  SELECT last_name
  FROM customer_contacts
);
```

The data remaining in the myminus table is the same result that you would have achieved using a MINUS operator on the two queries.

Performing an INTERSECT

To simulate an INTERSECT using a temporary table, first create a new table using the first query to define the columns and populate the initial data rows.

```
CREATE TEMPORARY TABLE myminus AS
SELECT first_name FROM customer_contacts;
```

Then delete the rows that do not also appear in the second query using a subquery and the NOT IN operator, as follows:

```
DELETE FROM myminus
WHERE first_name NOT IN (
  SELECT last_name
  FROM customer_contacts
);
```

The data remaining in the myminus table is the same result that you would have achieved using an INTERSECT operator on the two queries.

Summary

In this lesson, you learned how to combine the results from different queries using the UNION operator, and how to simulate the MINUS and INTERSECT operations in MySQL. In the next lesson, you will learn how to manage database tables.

LESSON 14

Creating and Modifying Tables

In this lesson, you learn how to use the SQL commands for managing tables and databases in MySQL. This subset of SQL is known as the Data Definition Language.

Before we look at how tables are managed in MySQL, we should examine the command set that is used to create databases on a MySQL server.

Creating a New Database

You use the CREATE DATABASE command to create a new database. To create a new database named newdb, issue the following command. The output will be as shown if the database is created successfully.

```
mysql> CREATE DATABASE newdb;
Query OK, 1 row affected (0.02 sec)
```

 Creating Databases   Usually you execute this command when you are connected as the root user, but you can create databases when logged in as any user who has the CREATE privilege. You will learn more about the privilege system in MySQL in Lesson 18, "Managing User Access."

The database name can be up to 64 characters in length and can contain any character that is allowed in a directory name on your underlying operating system, except for the / and \ characters. The database name also cannot be one of the SQL reserved words listed in Appendix F, "MySQL Reserved Words," which can be found on the book's website at www. samspublishing.com.

The database name must be unique as well. If you attempt to issue a CREATE DATABASE statement for a database that already exists, you will see an error. The following output is produced when you attempt to create newdb for a second time:

```
mysql> CREATE DATABASE newdb;
ERROR 1007 (HY000): Can't create database 'newdb';
database exists
```

The optional attribute IF NOT EXISTS can be added to a CREATE DATABASE statement to avoid an error if the database already exists. Instead, a warning is generated, which you can view using the SHOW WARNINGS command.

```
mysql> CREATE DATABASE IF NOT EXISTS newdb;
Query OK, 0 rows affected, 1 warning (0.00 sec)

mysql> SHOW WARNINGS;
+-------+------+-------------------------------------------------+
| Level | Code | Message                                         |
+-------+------+-------------------------------------------------+
| Note  | 1007 | Can't create database 'newdb'; database exists  |
+-------+------+-------------------------------------------------+
1 row in set (0.00 sec)
```

Because a warning is generated instead of an error, you can use this technique in a batch script that contains a series of SQL commands to set up a database; the script will continue on to the next command if the database already exists.

Character Sets and Collations

MySQL supports different character sets and collations to provide functionality for users who want to create database applications in different languages.

The character set determines how MySQL stores character data. Each letter in a character string is represented internally by a numeric value, and the character set determines the character mapping of each number.

A collation is a set of rules for comparing characters in a character set—essentially, it defines the alphabetical order for a character set. For instance, the character ö in a German character set is usually treated as OE for ordering purposes.

Collation rules can also take into account case sensitivity. You saw in Lesson 7, "String Operators and Functions," that string comparisons are not case sensitive unless you include the BINARY keyword. In fact, BINARY is a collation type that tells MySQL to consider the underlying character map values. The default collation for MySQL is not case sensitive, so it considers the character P to have the same value as p when ordering.

The actual character sets available on your system depend on those supported by your operating system. To see the character sets available, issue the SHOW CHARACTER SET command. The following output shows just a few sample lines of output—your actual output will vary.

```
mysql> SHOW CHARACTER SET;
+---------+-------------------+-------------------+--------+
| Charset | Description       | Default collation | Maxlen |
+---------+-------------------+-------------------+--------+
| ascii   | US ASCII          | ascii_general_ci  |      1 |
| hebrew  | ISO 8859-8 Hebrew | hebrew_general_ci |      1 |
| ujis    | EUC-JP Japanese   | ujis_japanese_ci  |      3 |
| greek   | ISO 8859-7 Greek  | greek_general_ci  |      1 |
...
```

The Maxlen column indicates the number of bytes required to store a character using each character set. Some complex alphabets require 2 or 3 bytes per character.

To specify the default character set and collation for a new database, use the CHARACTER SET and COLLATION attributes in the CREATE DATABASE statement. For instance, the following statement would create a new database using a Greek character set and the greek_general_ci collation:

```
mysql> CREATE DATABASE greekdb
    -> CHARACTER SET greek COLLATE greek_general_ci;
Query OK, 1 row affected (0.00 sec)
```

 Collation If you do not specify a collation with the COLLATE keyword, the default collation for a character set—as shown in the output from SHOW CHARACTER SET—will be used.

Altering a Database

The ALTER DATABASE statement enables you to change the characteristics of an existing database. Its syntax is the same as the syntax of the CREATE DATABASE statement, and any CHARACTER SET or COLLATE specification changes the behavior of an existing database.

For example, suppose you want to change greekdb to use the ASCII character set. You would issue the following command:

```
mysql> ALTER DATABASE greekdb
    -> CHARACTER SET ascii;
Query OK, 1 row affected (0.00 sec)
```

Dropping a Database

Use the DROP DATABASE command to drop a database completely. Use this command with extreme caution—you cannot recover a dropped database unless you have a backup.

Dropping Databases   A user must have the DROP privilege in order to drop a database. Grant this privilege sparingly.

To drop the greekdb database, issue the following command:

```
mysql> DROP DATABASE greekdb;
Query OK, 0 rows affected (0.00 sec)
```

Similar to CREATE DATABASE IF NOT EXISTS, you can use DROP DATABASE IF EXISTS to suppress an error if you try to drop a nonexistent database.

Managing Tables

Now let's look at how database tables are defined, altered, and dropped.

Creating a New Table

Use the CREATE TABLE command to create a new database table. A table definition consists of a number of columns and a set of table options. Each column in the table definition is given a *data type* and can also be given a *constraint*.

A column name can be up to 64 characters long and can contain any character. You must enclose the column name in quotes (") or backticks (`) if it contains a space. A column name cannot be one of the keywords listed in Appendix F.

The data type of a column determines what values it can hold and the maximum size of a stored value. For instance, a column defined as VARCHAR(6) can contain text data up to 6 characters in length. You will learn more about the MySQL data types in Lesson 16, "Designing Your Database."

A column constraint is used to impose a restriction on the values stored in that column. For example, a column defined as UNIQUE may not contain the same value more than once. If a constraint is violated when you attempt an INSERT or UPDATE on the table, MySQL will return an error and your SQL statement will fail.

Let's look at an example from the sample database. The following statement creates the products table:

```
CREATE TABLE products (
    product_code   VARCHAR(10)    PRIMARY KEY,
    name           VARCHAR(40)    NOT NULL UNIQUE,
    weight         DECIMAL(6,2)   NOT NULL,
    price          DECIMAL(6,2)   NOT NULL
);
```

Although the formatting shown in this example is not necessary, it helps to show the different elements of the column specification. You give the column a name, then its data type, and then any constraints that are required.

 CREATE TABLE   The CREATE TABLE statement has many different options, and there is not space in this chapter to cover them all. Please refer to the online MySQL manual at http://dev.mysql.com/doc/refman/5.0/en/create-table.html for the full CREATE TABLE syntax.

In this table, the product_code column is defined as a 10-character string and is the PRIMARY KEY for the table. Each table may have only one PRIMARY KEY because this is a unique identifier for each row of the table. You will learn more about keys in Lesson 17, "Keys and Indexes."

 Primary Keys   A PRIMARY KEY field also has the UNIQUE and NOT NULL constraints, even if you do not specify them in the CREATE TABLE statement.

The other three columns are given the NOT NULL constraint. With this constraint, any attempt to insert data rows where any of these columns are left empty will fail.

NULLs NULL means no value. It is not the same as 0 or an empty string. Therefore, it is possible for the name column to contain '', and for the weight and price columns to contain 0.00.

The name column is a text field with a maximum length of 40 characters; it is specified as UNIQUE. This is done to ensure that two products in the database will never have exactly the same name.

The weight and price columns are defined as DECIMAL(6,2). This is a 6-digit number with 2 of those digits appearing after the decimal point. Therefore, the maximum value is 9999.99.

Data Types Refer to Appendix D, "MySQL Data Type Reference," which can be found on the book's website at www.samspublishing.com for a complete list of data types that can be used for a column definition.

Specifying Default Values

You can give each column a default value using the DEFAULT keyword. Then whenever a row is inserted without explicitly giving a value for that column, the default value will be used.

This statement creates a simple table in which the value of the sex column will be Female unless you specify otherwise.

```
mysql> CREATE TABLE people (
    ->    name VARCHAR(40),
    ->    sex VARCHAR(6) DEFAULT 'Female'
    -> );
Query OK, 0 rows affected (0.00 sec)
```

Then insert a row that gives a value for only the name column, as follows. You will learn how to form an INSERT statement in Lesson 15, "Working with Data."

```
mysql> INSERT INTO people (name)
    -> VALUES ('Jane Doe');
Query OK, 1 row affected (0.00 sec)
```

Retrieving the data from this table shows that the default value was used:

```
mysql> SELECT * FROM people;
+-----------+---------+
| name      | sex     |
+-----------+---------+
| Jane Doe  | Female  |
+-----------+---------+
1 row in set (0.00 sec)
```

 Default Values If there is a default value for a column, it will be displayed in the Default column of the output from the DESCRIBE command.

Autoincrementing Columns

It is possible to specify a column in a table as an autoincrementing column. Such a column will contain a number that is assigned automatically each time a new row is inserted. To do this, use the AUTO_INCREMENT attribute on a numeric column.

The orders table in the sample database uses AUTO_INCREMENT on the order_id column to assign a new order number each time an order is placed. The table definition is as follows:

```
CREATE TABLE orders (
  order_id       INT           PRIMARY KEY AUTO_INCREMENT,
  customer_code  VARCHAR(10)   NOT NULL,
  order_date     DATE          NOT NULL
);
```

If you insert a new record into this table without giving a value for the order_id column, its value will be assigned as the next unused number in sequence.

```
mysql> INSERT INTO orders (customer_code, order_date)
    -> VALUES ('SCICORP', '2006-03-20');
Query OK, 1 row affected (0.00 sec)
```

The following query selects the two most recently added records from the orders table. As you can see, the newly inserted record has an order_id that is one higher than the previous record.

```
mysql> SELECT * FROM orders
    -> ORDER BY order_id DESC
    -> LIMIT 2;
+----------+---------------+------------+
| order_id | customer_code | order_date |
+----------+---------------+------------+
|        8 | SCICORP       | 2006-03-20 |
|        7 | MUSGRP        | 2006-02-02 |
+----------+---------------+------------+
2 rows in set (0.00 sec)
```

 Autoincrement Columns   If a column has the AUTO_INCREMENT property, this will be shown in the Extras column of the output from the DESCRIBE command.

Temporary Tables

A temporary table lasts only for the current MySQL session. Therefore, after you have disconnected from the database, the table will no longer be available after you reconnect. To create a temporary table, use CREATE TEMPORARY TABLE instead of CREATE TABLE.

Temporary tables are useful if you need to manipulate data using temporary storage within an application and you do not want the tables you use to remain on the system when you are finished with them.

A temporary table name can be used simultaneously in multiple MySQL sessions. Therefore, if two instances of your program run at the same time, it is not necessary to generate a unique name for the temporary table in each instance.

Using a Query to Create a Table

You can use the result of a query to create a new table by putting a SELECT statement inside the CREATE TABLE command.

The following example creates a table that contains a subset of the customer_contacts table for one customer. This is also created as a temporary table, so it will be destroyed when you end your MySQL sessions.

```
mysql> CREATE TEMPORARY TABLE scicorp_customers AS
    -> SELECT * FROM customer_contacts
    -> WHERE customer_code = 'SCICORP';
Query OK, 4 rows affected (0.01 sec)
Records: 4  Duplicates: 0  Warnings: 0
```

The keyword AS is optional but can be included to make the command more readable. If you view the structure of the new table, you will see that all the columns from customer_contacts are present.

```
mysql> DESC scicorp_customers;
+---------------+-------------+------+-----+---------+-------+
| Field         | Type        | Null | Key | Default | Extra |
+---------------+-------------+------+-----+---------+-------+
| contact_id    | int(11)     | NO   |     | 0       |       |
| customer_code | varchar(10) | NO   |     |         |       |
| first_name    | varchar(30) | NO   |     |         |       |
| last_name     | varchar(30) | NO   |     |         |       |
| email         | text        | YES  |     | NULL    |       |
| telephone     | text        | YES  |     | NULL    |       |
+---------------+-------------+------+-----+---------+-------+
6 rows in set (0.00 sec)
```

Notice, however, that the contact_id column is no longer a PRIMARY KEY for the table and is not an AUTO_INCREMENT column. Keys are not copied when you create a table using this method, but MySQL does retain the data types of the columns and any NOT NULL constraints.

Storage Engines

MySQL supports several different storage engines that are used to handle different table types. The storage engine can be specified in the CREATE TABLE statement using the ENGINE keyword to tell MySQL how a table should be handled.

The default storage engine for MySQL is called MyISAM. Using this handler, tables are stored on disk in three files, with extensions .MYI, .MYD, and .frm. An alternative disk-based table handler is InnoDB, which supports some features that are not available in MyISAM such as transactions that you will learn about in Lesson 15. Support for InnoDB must be enabled at compile-time for your MySQL server.

The MEMORY storage engine is a very fast storage engine that stores tables in memory only. However, because no data is written to disk, the contents of your tables are destroyed when the MySQL server is stopped. MEMORY is usually used for temporary tables.

The following example creates a new table that uses the InnoDB engine:

```
CREATE TABLE mytable (
  id INTEGER PRIMARY KEY,
  name TEXT
) ENGINE=InnoDB;
```

When using a query to create a table, the ENGINE keyword must appear before the query. The following statement uses the MEMORY engine for a temporary table that is created from a query:

```
CREATE TEMPORARY TABLE presinc_orders
ENGINE=MEMORY
SELECT * FROM orders
WHERE customer_code = 'PRESINC';
```

Altering Tables

You can use the ALTER TABLE command to change part of a table definition. You can ADD, MODIFY, or DROP a column on a live table, although, of course, you should take care to ensure that doing so will not cause errors in an application or query that relies on the existing table structure.

To add a new column, use the ADD keyword followed by a column definition. For example, the following statement adds a new column named fax to the customer_contacts table, which has a maximum length of 12 characters:

```
mysql> ALTER TABLE customer_contacts
    -> ADD fax VARCHAR(12);
Query OK, 11 rows affected (0.00 sec)
Records: 11  Duplicates: 0  Warnings: 0
```

To modify an existing column, use the MODIFY keyword followed by the existing column name, a new column name, and a column definition. You can use MODIFY both to rename a column and to change its definition.

Suppose you realize that the fax column is not long enough to store international fax numbers, so you want to make this an unlimited-length TEXT type column. The following statement changes the data type of fax. Notice that the column name appears twice in this statement because you do not want to change its name.

```
mysql> ALTER TABLE customer_contacts
    -> CHANGE fax fax TEXT;
Query OK, 11 rows affected (0.01 sec)
Records: 11  Duplicates: 0  Warnings: 0
```

To drop a column from a table, use the DROP keyword followed by the column name. The following statement drops the fax column from the customer_contacts table:

```
mysql> ALTER TABLE customer_contacts
    -> DROP fax;
Query OK, 11 rows affected (0.00 sec)
Records: 11  Duplicates: 0  Warnings: 0
```

Dropping Tables

To drop a table, use the DROP TABLE command followed by the name of the table. Beware that a dropped table cannot be recovered unless you have a backup.

To drop the people table you created earlier in this lesson, use the following command:

```
mysql> DROP TABLE people;
Query OK, 0 rows affected (0.00 sec)
```

You can use DROP TABLE IF EXISTS so that no error occurs if a table does not exist. This is useful in a batch script that creates all the tables for a database: The script will delete the existing tables before re-creating them but will not fall over if the tables do not exist yet.

Summary

In this lesson, you learned how to use the Data Definition Language to create and modify databases and tables in MySQL. In the next lesson, you will learn how to use the Data Manipulation Language to work with data.

LESSON 15
Working with Data

In this lesson, you learn how to use the INSERT, UPDATE, and DELETE SQL statements to manage data rows in your MySQL tables and load data from files.

The INSERT Statement

The subset of SQL that enables you to insert data and to update and delete existing records in a table is known as the Data Manipulation Language.

The INSERT statement adds a new row of data to a table. At its simplest, INSERT is followed by a table name, the keyword VALUES, and a list of values in parentheses that correspond to each column in the table in turn.

The products table contains four columns—product_code, name, price, and weight—so you can insert a new product using the following statement:

```
mysql> INSERT INTO products
    -> VALUES ('NEWPROD', 'A new product', 19.99, 3.5);
Query OK, 1 row affected (0.02 sec)
```

The response from MySQL indicates that a row has been successfully inserted.

 INTO The INTO keyword is actually optional. However, you will usually see it included in INSERT statements because it makes them more readable.

The second INSERT format requires you to specify the name of each column before giving the values—this is known as a full insert. The following statement works the same way as the previous example:

```
mysql> INSERT INTO products (product_code, name, price, weight)
    -> VALUES ('NEWPROD2', 'Another new product', 29.99, 5.2);
Query OK, 1 row affected (0.02 sec)
```

This might seem a little long-winded, but it means that you do not need to give a value for every column in the table, or list the values in the correct order. One big advantage is that if the table structure changes, the second example in this section will still work, whereas the first example will fail because every column in the table is not given a value.

Column Mismatch If you try to execute an INSERT statement with the wrong number of columns, whether or not you use a full insert, MySQL will give an error and the insert will fail.

Notice that the second example used a different product_code value than the first. This is because product_code is a PRIMARY KEY column and can contain only unique values. If you try to perform an insert that violates a database constraint, you will see an error like the following:

```
mysql> INSERT INTO products
    -> VALUES ('NEWPROD', 'A new product', 19.99, 3.5);
ERROR 1062 (23000): Duplicate entry 'NEWPROD' for key 1
```

Default Column Values

When you use a full insert, any columns that are not listed have their default value inserted for the new data row, or NULL if there is no default. A column that has the AUTO_INCREMENT property is assigned the next number in sequence by default.

NULL Columns If you do not give a value for a column that has the NOT NULL constraint and also does not have a default value, the insert will fail.

If you explicitly want to use a column's default value in an INSERT statement, use the DEFAULT keyword as its value. In the following examples, you insert new record into the orders table, where the order_id column has the AUTO_INCREMENT property:

```
mysql> INSERT INTO orders
    -> (order_id, customer_code, order_date)
    -> VALUES (DEFAULT, 'MUSGRP', '2006-04-01');
Query OK, 1 row affected (0.01 sec)

mysql> INSERT INTO orders (customer_code, order_date)
    -> VALUES ('MUSGRP', '2006-04-01');
Query OK, 1 row affected (0.00 sec)
```

Both formats of the INSERT statement perform the same job. You can then query the orders table to verify that the two records were inserted with sequential order_id values.

Inserting Multiple Rows

You can insert several rows in a single INSERT statement by supplying multiple lists of values. Each list must be enclosed in parentheses and separated by a comma.

The following statement inserts three new rows into the customers table:

```
mysql> INSERT INTO customers (customer_code, name)
    -> VALUES
    -> ('ACME', 'ACME Enterprises'),
    -> ('BLOGGS', 'Bloggs and Company'),
    -> ('CORPLTD', 'Corporation Limited');
Query OK, 3 rows affected (0.00 sec)
Records: 3  Duplicates: 0  Warnings: 0
```

If one of the rows in a multiple INSERT statement causes an error (for instance, a duplicate value in a UNIQUE column), the insert will fail. The values are inserted in sequence, however, so rows before the one that caused the error will have already been inserted into the database.

Atomic transactions—database operations that all take place at the same time—are discussed in the "Transactions in MySQL" section later in this lesson.

Using a Query to Insert Rows

Instead of supplying a list of values as the data for a new row, you can use the result of a query to insert one or more rows into a table.

The format for this type of INSERT command uses a SELECT statement in place of VALUES. The requirements of an INSERT must hold true: The query must return the correct number of columns for the insert, and the insert must not violate any column constraints.

The following query inserts a new contact for each customer named Joe Soap. This is a trivial example, but it demonstrates how this feature can be used with powerful results.

```
mysql> INSERT INTO customer_contacts
    -> (customer_code, first_name, last_name)
    -> SELECT customer_code, 'Joe', 'Soap'
    -> FROM customers;
Query OK, 6 rows affected (0.00 sec)
Records: 6  Duplicates: 0  Warnings: 0
```

A new row in customer_contacts is inserted for each row in the customers table. The customer_code column is populated from the customer_code value in customers, whereas first_name and last_name are given static values; these are returned as is by the query and, therefore, are used as fixed values in the insert.

The contact_id column in customer_contacts is an AUTO_INCREMENT column, so it is automatically assigned sequential numbers for each row inserted by this statement.

The DELETE Statement

The DELETE statement is used to remove data rows from a table. Its syntax is similar to a SELECT statement: You supply a table name after the keyword FROM and use a WHERE clause to filter the rows that are to be deleted.

 Deleting Without a WHERE clause, DELETE deletes every rows from the given table. Unless this is the result you want, always make sure that you include a WHERE clause in a DELETE statement.

To delete only a single row from a table, you should ensure that the WHERE clause will match only that row. Usually, you should check the value of the table's PRIMARY KEY column to ensure that an exact match is found.

The following example deletes one of the new products that you inserted in the previous section:

```
mysql> DELETE FROM products
    -> WHERE product_code = 'NEWPROD';
Query OK, 1 row affected (0.00 sec)
```

The response from the DELETE command indicates the number of rows that were removed. The following example deletes several rows from the customer_contacts table using a WHERE clause that finds all the customers with a given name. These rows will be the ones inserted in the section "Using a Query to Insert Rows."

```
mysql> DELETE FROM customer_contacts
    -> WHERE first_name = 'Joe'
    -> AND last_name = 'Soap';
Query OK, 6 rows affected (0.00 sec)
```

A DELETE cannot be undone unless it is part of a transaction that is rolled back. You will learn about this feature in the "Transactions in MySQL" section later in this lesson.

The UPDATE Statement

The UPDATE statement is used to change one or some of the values in a data row. As with DELETE, you include a WHERE clause to indicate that this row or rows are to be updated.

 Updating Without a WHERE clause, UPDATE performs the same update on every row in the table. Unless this is the result you want, always include a WHERE clause in an UPDATE statement.

You specify the values to be changed in a list after the SET keyword, separated with commas. The following example updates the name and price of an existing product:

```
mysql> UPDATE products
    -> SET name = 'Large product (new and improved)',
    ->     price = 23.99
    -> WHERE product_code = 'MAXI';
Query OK, 1 row affected (0.02 sec)
Rows matched: 1  Changed: 1  Warnings: 0
```

The response from MySQL confirms that the update was successful and reports that one row was changed. The numbers against Rows matched and Changed in the output might be different: The former tells you how many data rows were matched by the WHERE clause, whereas the latter indicates how many were altered from their previous value.

If you were to issue the previous statement again, you would see this output instead because the column values are already the same as the values in the UPDATE statement:

```
Query OK, 0 rows affected (0.01 sec)
Rows matched: 1  Changed: 0  Warnings: 0
```

Alternative INSERT Syntax   MySQL enables you to use a similar syntax to UPDATE for INSERT statements, so you can say INSERT INTO table SET col1 = 'val1', SET col2 = ... This is particularly useful when you are generating SQL statements from a client application for either an INSERT or an UPDATE, depending on whether the data row exists yet.

Using this method, you need to generate the keyword at the beginning of the statement and specify a WHERE clause only if it is an UPDATE to change its behavior.

Updating with a Derived Column

You can use a calculation, function, or even subquery as the value in an UPDATE statement. The following is a simple example that adds 10% to every price in the products table:

```
mysql> UPDATE products
    -> SET price = price * 1.10;
Query OK, 3 rows affected, 3 warnings (0.00 sec)
Rows matched: 3  Changed: 3  Warnings: 3
```

This statement does not require a WHERE clause because you want the calculation to apply to every row in the table. MySQL calculates the value of price * 1.10 for each row in the table and uses that value to update the corresponding row.

The following example uses a subquery to set the prices for each product based on its popularity. Each item's price will be set to $10 plus 10¢ for each time the product has been ordered.

```
mysql> UPDATE products p
    -> SET price = 10 + (
    ->   SELECT SUM(quantity) * 0.10
    ->   FROM order_lines o
    ->   WHERE o.product_code = p.product_code
    -> );
Query OK, 0 rows affected, 1 warning (0.00 sec)
Rows matched: 3  Changed: 3  Warnings: 1
```

Examining the products table will show that the prices have been updated and that each has a different value.

```
mysql> SELECT * FROM products;
+--------------+-----------------------------+--------+-------+
| product_code | name                        | weight | price |
+--------------+-----------------------------+--------+-------+
| MINI         | Small product               |   1.50 | 13.60 |
| MIDI         | Medium product              |   4.50 | 11.00 |
| MAXI         | Large product (new formula) |   8.00 | 14.80 |
+--------------+-----------------------------+--------+-------+
3 rows in set (0.00 sec)
```

 Updating with a Subquery   Just as when you use a subquery in a filter, a subquery used to perform an insert must return only one row and one column. Otherwise, MySQL gives an error.

The REPLACE Statement

The REPLACE statement works just like INSERT, except that if a row already exists in the table with the same PRIMARY KEY value as the new data, the new row replaces it. Therefore, REPLACE never causes a PRIMARY KEY violation.

The syntax for REPLACE is just like INSERT, or you can use the alternative syntax with SET, if you prefer. The following examples both perform the same operation: to replace the MINI product with a new description, weight, and price.

```
mysql> REPLACE INTO products
    -> (product_code, name, weight, price)
    -> VALUES ('MINI', 'Mini produt', '1.25', 3.99);
Query OK, 2 rows affected (0.00 sec)
```

```
mysql> REPLACE INTO products
    -> SET product_code = 'MINI',
    ->     name = 'Mini product',
    ->     weight = 1.25,
    ->     price = 3.99;
Query OK, 2 rows affected (0.00 sec)
```

Replacing Rows   The actual behavior of REPLACE is to execute a DELETE operation with the given primary key value and then perform an INSERT; it does not perform an UPDATE.

The output from the previous examples shows two rows affected because two operations took place: one DELETE and one INSERT.

Loading Data from a File

You can load data from an external file into MySQL using the LOAD DATA INFILE command. The data in your file must be in a structured format—the default format is one record on each line, with values separated by tabs.

The file shown in Listing 15.1 contains a file that could be loaded into the products table using the following command:

```
LOAD DATA INFILE '/home/chris/listing15.1.txt'
INTO TABLE products;
```

LISTING 15.1   Sample Tab-Separated Data File

```
BLUE    Blue product    3.0    13.99
RED     Red product     3.5    25.00
GREEN   Green product   4.5    6.50
```

 Paths   If no path is given for the filename in LOAD DATA INFILE, MySQL looks for it in the MySQL system directory.

The previous command works because the columns in the data file map precisely to the columns in the products table. If you instead needed to specify the columns because the data file values were in a different order or some were omitted, you could do this by giving a list of columns in parentheses at the end of the command.

The following statement is identical to the previous example, using a full insert in the LOAD DATA INFILE statement:

```
LOAD DATA INFILE '/home/chris/mysql10/listing15.1.txt'
INTO TABLE products
(product_code, name, weight, price);
```

If your data file is not tab-separated, you must specify the separation method in the LOAD DATA INFILE statement using the TERMINATED BY and ENCLOSED BY keywords.

Supposing that you have a comma-separated data file with each value enclosed in quotes, you would use the following command to indicate the separation:

```
LOAD DATA INFILE '/home/chris/mysql10/listing15.1.txt'
INTO TABLE products
FIELDS TERMINATED BY ',' ENCLOSED BY '"'
(product_code, name, weight, price);
```

 Line Terminators   If your data file does not use the newline character to separate records, you can specify the line terminator using LINES STARTING BY and TERMINATED BY.

Sometimes you will be working with a data file that contains one or more header lines. Often when you extract data from another program, the first line of the output contains the column names used in that program. Listing 15.2 shows an example of a comma-separated data file that includes a line of headings.

LISTING 15.2   Comma-Separated Data File with Column Headings

```
"ProdCode","ProdName","ProdWeight","ProdPrice"
"BLUE","Blue product",3.0,13.99
"RED","Red product",3.5 ,25.00
"GREEN","Green product",4.5 ,6.50
```

To ignore one or more lines at the top of a data file, use the IGNORE keyword followed by the number of lines and the LINES keyword—you must use the plural LINES even if you want to skip only one line. The following statement successfully loads only the data records from Listing 15.2:

```
LOAD DATA INFILE '/home/chris/mysql10/products.txt'
INTO TABLE products
FIELDS TERMINATED BY ',' ENCLOSED BY '"'
IGNORE 1 LINES
(product_code, name, weight, price)
```

Why Use Transactions?

A transaction is a group of Database Manipulation Language statements that occur as a unit. Either the entire transaction takes place and is committed to the database, or none of the attempted changes is saved.

Transactions enable you to ensure data integrity when performing multiple database operations. Consider a product database that includes the number of each item in stock. When a customer places an order, a record is inserted into the orders table for each product ordered, and the corresponding stock levels are decreased.

Both of these changes to the database need to take place in a single transaction. Otherwise, two possible pitfalls could be encountered.

If the items are added to a customer's order before the stock levels are decreased, there will be a period of time—albeit usually only a fraction of a second—during which another database user could query the stock levels of a product and see the wrong value.

Although both of these pitfalls are extremely uncommon, the severity of the data corruption if one occurs—particularly where financial data is involved—means that transactions are essential to make sure both actions happen as a unit.

Transactions in MySQL

Transactions in MySQL are available only on tables that use the InnoDB or BDB storage engines. See Lesson 14, "Creating and Modifying Tables," for more information on how to select a specific table handler.

To begin a transaction, issue the BEGIN TRANSACTION command. Any database-manipulation statements issued after that command form part of the same transaction.

Until you issue a statement that ends a transaction, the effects of any commands that you enter are visible only within the current MySQL session. For instance, if you delete rows from a table after issuing the START TRANSACTION command, other database users can still query those rows, even though in your session they appear to be already deleted.

To commit all the changes made in a transaction, issue the COMMIT command. Doing so causes each INSERT, UPDATE, and DELETE statement that forms part of the transaction to be executed immediately and as one unit.

Autocommit Mode

By default, the system variable AUTOCOMMIT is set to 1, which instructs MySQL to process each database-manipulation statement issued immediately as a single transaction. This is the behavior you have already seen, with an INSERT, UPDATE, or DELETE committed to the database as soon as you issue the command.

Consider this simple UPDATE statement:

```
UPDATE PRODUCTS
SET price = 5.99
WHERE code = 'MINI';
```

When autocommit mode is turned on, the previous statement is executed as if you had entered the following:

```
BEGIN TRANSACTION;

UPDATE PRODUCTS
SET price = 5.99
WHERE code = 'MINI';

COMMIT;
```

By setting the value of AUTOCOMMIT to 0, you disable this feature so that you have to use COMMIT to store any changes made—or use ROLLBACK to discard changes—since the beginning of the transaction.

To disable AUTOCOMMIT, use the SET command as shown:

```
mysql> SET AUTOCOMMIT=0;
Query OK, 0 rows affected (0.00 sec)
```

Rolling Back a Transaction

You can also end a transaction without committing the changes with the ROLLBACK command. The result is that the database state is rolled back to how it was before you issued the START TRANSACTION command.

The following example shows how you can recover from a disastrously wrong DELETE statement—remember to always include the WHERE clause—if it occurs within a transaction:

```
mysql> START TRANSACTION;
Query OK, 0 rows affected (0.00 sec)

mysql> DELETE FROM products;
Query OK, 3 rows affected (0.03 sec)

mysql> ROLLBACK;
Query OK, 0 rows affected (0.01 sec)
```

If you then query the products table, you will see that it still contains records.

Transactional Table Handlers   If you try to use transactions with tables that do not use the InnoDB storage engine, MySQL will not give an error when you START TRANSACTION.

In the previous example, there would be a warning that ROLLBACK could not be used, but at this point it is already too late to undo the DELETE command.

Summary

In this lesson, you learned how to use the Database Manipulation Language in MySQL and how to use transactions to ensure data integrity. In the next lesson, we discuss some of the factors to consider when designing a new database.

Lesson 16

Designing Your Database

In this lesson, we discuss some of the factors that you should consider when designing a database.

Relationships

Now that you know how to create database tables and manipulate data, it's time to take a look at the principles of relational databases and see how to apply good design practices to your own databases.

Data in a relational database is split across several tables in a structured way. Relationships are the rules that determine how data in one table is related to data in another. When you join tables in SQL, you specify the relationship between the tables in the query. Refer to Lesson 11, "Joining Tables," for more information on joins.

Consider the relationship between two tables in the sample database. The orders table is related to customers. Each record in the orders table contains a customer_id, which is a foreign key column that corresponds to the primary key in customers.

The relationship between customers and orders is known as a *one-to-many* relationship because one row in the customers table can be related to many rows in the orders table. Think of what the database is trying to achieve here—a customer must not be limited to placing only one order!

Many-to-One   A one-to-many relationship could be considered a many-to-one relationship, depending on which way you look at it. You could think of the relationship between products and customers as many-to-one.

The relationship between products and orders is a *many-to-many* relationship. An order can contain the same product many times—although the quantity column should help to avoid the need to do this—and, of course, each product can appear on many orders.

In the sample table, the many-to-many relationship between products and orders is actually implemented using two separate relationships and the order_lines table. There is a one-to-many relationship between orders and order_lines, and also a one-to-many relationship between products and order_lines.

As you might expect, a one-to-one relationship is also possible, although there is no relationship of this kind in the sample database. A one-to-one relationship uses a key that is unique in both tables; therefore, the data could actually be stored in one table instead of two.

Usually you use a one-to-one relationship for performance reasons. For example, you could keep one table highly optimized by storing only the most commonly used columns. The second table would contain larger amounts of data and would be joined to the first only when those columns were required. In particular, you can often improve performance by separating large text or binary data columns from the body of a table using a one-to-one relationship.

Normalization

Normalization is the process of optimizing the relationships between tables in your database. The process involves several stages of splitting a database into smaller components and adding the appropriate relationships.

Many reasons exist for normalizing your database from the outset. Normalization helps to improve the performance of the database by using only the most efficient relationships between tables. It also improves maintainability by reducing repetitive data.

The first stage of normalization involves eliminating any columns that might contain multiple values. For example, consider the following table. This shows a variation on the customers table that also includes the data that is in the customer_contacts table.

customer_code	name	contacts
PRESINC	Presidents Incorporated	Abraham Lincoln, Richard Nixon, Franklin Roosevelt, Theordore Roosevelt
SCICORP	Science Corporation	Albert Einstein, Charles Darwin, Marie Curie, Benjamin Franklin
MUSGRP	Musicians of America	George Gershwin, Benjamin Britten, John Lennon

FIGURE 16.1   A table with multiple values in a column.

As you can see, the contacts column contains multiple names, separated using commas. This type of table structure must be eliminated.

Notice also that this structure enables you to store only a contact name. Another approach is to have one row in the customers table per contact. This satisfies the requirement of not having multiple values in a column, but this structure will include a lot of duplicated data, as shown in Figure 16.2.

customer_code	name	contact_name	contract_email
PRESINC	Presidents Incorporated	Abraham Lincoln	lincoln@presidentsinc.com
PRESINC	Presidents Incorporated	Richard Nixon	nixon@presidentsinc.com
PRESINC	Presidents Incorporated	Franklin Roosevelt	fdr@presidentsinc.com
PRESINC	Presidents Incorporated	Theodore Roosevelt	roosevelt@presidnetsinc.com
SCICORP	Science Corporation	Albert Einstein	einstein@sciencecorp.com
SCICORP	Science Corporation	Charles Darwin	darwin@sciencecorp.com
SCICORP	Science Corporation	Marie Curie	curie@sciencecorp.com
SCICORP	Science Corporation	Benjamin Franklin	franklin@sciencecorp.com
MUSGRP	Musicians of America	George Gershwin	gershwin@musgrp.com
MUSGRP	Musicians of America	Benjamin Britten	britten@musgrp.com
MUSGRP	Musicians of America	John Lennon	lennon@musgrp.com

FIGURE 16.2   A table with duplicated data.

One major pitfall with this approach is that it is possible for some of the contacts for a customer to have different name values than others. There is no need for the company name to be duplicated in this table; the next stage of normalization will eliminate this.

You should remove duplicate rows by creating a related table; this is how the customers and customer_contacts tables are constructed in the sample database you have been following in this book.

The customer_code column is a primary key for customers and a foreign key for customer_contacts, with a one-to-many relationship. This structure ensures that each customer record appears only once in customers but that each customer_code can appear many times in customer_contacts; in this way, many contact names are added for each customer.

The normalized tables from this part of the database are shown in Figure 16.3.

customer_code	name
PRESINC	Presidents Incorporated
SCICORP	Science Corporation
MUSGRP	Musicians of America

contact_id	customer_code	first_name	last_name	email
1	PRESINC	Abraham	Lincoln	lincoln@presidentsinc.com
2	PRESINC	Richard	Nixon	nixon@presidentsinc.com
10	MUSGRP	Benjamin	Britten	britten@musgrp.com
11	MUSGRP	John	Lennon	lennon@musgrp.com

FIGURE 16.3   The properly normalized tables.

The contact_id column is included in customer_contacts as an auto-incrementing unique primary key for this table. We also decided to split the first_name and last_name columns in the final database.

Naming Tables and Columns

Now let's look at some of the database design issues to consider when creating tables in MySQL.

The names you give your tables and their columns are important—choose them carefully. First and foremost, the names you use should be clear identifiers. Table name should indicate what data is being stored, and column names should identify what their values represent.

For example, the `products` table does exactly what you would expect: It contains details of the products in the database. The purposes of columns named `weight` and `price` in this table are obvious as well.

You can adopt many different naming conventions. No one convention in particular is correct, and the one you choose to use will be a matter of preference, but you should try to retain a consistent naming scheme throughout your database.

In the sample database, table names are always plural (`customers`, `products`, and so on), but you might prefer to use singular nouns (such as `customer` and `product`) as the table names.

For both table names and column names, the sample database uses an underscore character to separate words, as in the `order_lines` table or the `product_code` column. Another popular convention is to capitalize the first letter of each word, as in `ProductCode` or sometimes `productCode`.

 Case Sensitivity   Table names in MySQL are usually case sensitive, so you must always use the same capitalization when referencing tables. On Windows systems and other platforms where the directory names on the file system are not case sensitive, table names are not case sensitive.

Column names are not case sensitive on any platform, but you should still try to keep a consistent capitalization to maintain readable code.

Sometimes you will come across systems in which the table identifiers contain a prefix or suffix to indicate that they are, in fact, a table, such as `tblProducts` or `products_tbl`. Other types of database objects might have their own naming scheme, such as an `idx` prefix or suffix for indexes. Column names might even contain a reference to the table name, such as prodWeight. These conventions sometimes aid the readability of an SQL statement by ensuring that the purpose of an identifier is absolutely clear.

Database and table identifier names can contain any character except ., \, and /. Because MySQL writes tables to disk using the names you provide, characters that can have special meanings in a filename are disallowed. A column name may use any character.

An identifier must be quoted if it contains a symbol character other than an underscore or is a reserved word. For a list of reserved words, refer to Appendix F, "MySQL Reserved Words," which can be found on the book's website at www.samspublishing.com. You quote an identifier by using the backtick (`) character.

For example, the following CREATE TABLE statement is perfectly valid—in practice, however, the poor choice of identifier names would render it unusable:

```
CREATE TABLE `table` (
    `a number` INT,
    `price$`   DECIMAL(6,2),
    `em@il`    TEXT,
    `varchar`  VARCHAR(1),
    `()`       INT
);
```

Data Types

When you create a new table, you must decide on the data types for each column. You already encountered some of the general column types, such as VARCHAR and INT, in Lesson 14. Now let's look at the most common data types in more detail.

Data Types   For a complete list of the data types you can use, refer to Appendix D, "MySQL Data Type Reference," which can be found on the book's website at www.samspublishing.com.

INTEGER

An integer is a whole number. The range of values that can be stored in an integer data type depends on the size of the integer—MySQL has five different sizes:

- TINYINT can store numbers from –128 to 127, or 0 to 255 if unsigned.

- SMALLINT can store numbers from –32,768 to 32,767, or 0 to 65,535 if unsigned.

- MEDIUMINT can store numbers from –8,388,608 to 8,388,607, or 0 to 16,777,215 if unsigned.

- INTEGER or INT can store numbers from –2,147,483,648 to 2,147,483,647, or 0 to 4,294,967,295 if unsigned.

- BIGINT can store numbers from –9,223,372,036,854,775,808 to 9,223,372,036,854,775,807, or 0 to 18,446,744,073,709,551,615 if unsigned.

Unsigned Values If an integer column is declared UNSIGNED, then it cannot store negative values. Doing so doubles the maximum values it can store.

In the sample database, quantity is defined as TINYINT UNSIGNED—it is expected that no single order will include more than 255 of the same product. The column is declared UNSIGNED because it is nonsense to allow a negative quantity.

DECIMAL

DECIMAL is an exact, fixed-point number. It is declared as DECIMAL(M,D), where M is the total number of digits and D is the number of digits after the decimal point.

In the sample database, we used DECIMAL for both the weight and price columns on the products table. Each was declared as DECIMAL(6,2), meaning that the largest value that could be stored in each is 9999.99—six numbers in total, with two appearing after the decimal point.

CHAR and VARCHAR

CHAR and VARCHAR are character data types. You give a maximum length in parentheses when specifying the column; if you attempt to insert a value longer than the maximum length, it is truncated.

A CHAR column has a fixed length, and values shorter than the maximum length are padded with spaces when stored. When you retrieve the value from a CHAR column, however, the trailing spaces are removed. The storage requirement for a CHAR column is simply 1 byte per character in the padded stored value.

A VARCHAR column has a variable length. Its storage requirement for each row depends on the length of the data item it contains—1 byte for each character is required, plus 1 byte that stores the value's length.

You might use a CHAR(2) column to store the two-letter state code in a person's address. In the sample database, we used VARCHAR(40) for a product's name. Forty characters should be more than enough.

 Maximum Lengths   You should always take care to ensure that a CHAR or VARCHAR is long enough for any data you can foresee the column holding. If you attempt to store a value longer than the maximum length, it will simply be truncated with no warning.

TEXT and BLOB

A BLOB is a binary large object that can contain a variable amount of data. TEXT is a similar data type for character data. Both types have the following variations:

- TINYTEXT and TINYBLOB have a maximum size of 255 bytes.

- TEXT and BLOB have a maximum size of 65,535 characters or bytes (64KB).

- MEDIUMTEXT and MEDIUMBLOB have a maximum size of 16,777,215 characters or bytes (16MB).

- LONGTEXT and LONGBLOB have a maximum size of 4,294,967,295 characters or bytes (4GB).

You can use a TEXT column to store free text data, such as a comments field. A BLOB column can be used to store true binary data, such as an image or sound clip, as well as free text data that you do not want to be stored using a character set.

DATE, DATETIME, and TIMESTAMP

The DATE data type in MySQL stores date values in the format YYYY-MM-DD. The DATETIME data type also includes a time element, in the format YYYY-DD-MM HH:MM:SS.

 Date Validation A date column does not perform any validation itself beyond checking that the format of a value meets the stated criteria. It is actually possible to store nonsense dates, such as 2005-02-29 or even 2005-99-99, in a date column.

The TIMESTAMP column type has a special property: Its value takes the current date and time whenever you insert a new row or update an existing row, unless you specify another value for the column.

TIMESTAMP columns are useful in tables for which you want an audit trail of when records were last inserted or updated. You do not need to build the time tracking into your application—simply let MySQL do the work.

Summary

In this lesson, you learned some of the principles of database design that you should apply in your own applications. In the next lesson, you will learn how to use indexes in MySQL.

LESSON 17

Keys and Indexes

In this lesson, you learn what indexes and keys are, and discover how indexing data on a key field can speed up data access times.

Understanding Keys and Indexes

The terms *keys* and *indexes* are often used interchangeably. A key column stores values that are used to filter rows in the table, either in the WHERE clause when querying that table or as part of a join to indicate the relationship between two tables.

A key column in MySQL is always indexed, but you can create an index on any table column or on multiple columns.

Primary Keys

Each table can contain only one primary key, which is a unique identifier for each row in the table. Often the primary key is an AUTO_INCREMENT column so that a new unique number is assigned automatically for each row added to the table.

You can be sure that when you query a table using a filter on a primary key field, MySQL will return only one row for each match in the filter.

An incremental ID number makes a good primary key. A unique character code—such as product_code in the sample products table—can work well, too, as long as you can ensure that the value will always be unique.

You should not use a person's name as a primary key because there is always a chance, however rare, that you could get a duplicate record. If you attempt to insert a duplicate value into a primary key column, a key violation occurs and MySQL gives an error.

Foreign Keys

A foreign key is a column that another table references. When you join two tables, the join condition usually is that the primary key from the first table must be equal to a foreign key in the second.

In the sample database, the foreign keys have the same name as the corresponding primary keys in their related tables. For instance, products. product_code is a primary key that is referenced by order_lines. product_code—each line of an order refers to exactly one product using a unique identifier for the product.

> **Foreign Key Constraints**   If you use the InnoDB table handler, you can add foreign key constraints at the database level to maintain referential integrity. You will learn how to do this in the section "Foreign Key Constraints with InnoDB," later in this chapter.

Indexes

Although there can be only one primary key on a table, you can create indexes on other columns in a table for performance reasons.

When MySQL searches for a value in a table column, if there is no index, it must start with the first row and check each row until it reaches the end of the table. However, when an index is available, the process is much quicker: The index tells MySQL where to look within the table for rows corresponding to that key value.

The more rows there are in a table, the bigger the impact a key can have on queries that return only a small number of rows from that table.

> **Selecting a Large Number of Rows**   If a query is intended to return the majority of the rows in a table, an index is not necessary and can often slow down a query.

You can define a column as a UNIQUE KEY if you are sure that its values will be unique. Queries using a UNIQUE KEY are faster than a non-unique key because MySQL knows that only one matching row will be returned from the table.

Using Indexes in MySQL

You can define a column that will be indexed in MySQL when you create a new table as a clause in the CREATE TABLE statement, or on an existing table using the CREATE INDEX command.

Defining Key Columns

You have already seen that the primary key on a table can be defined by adding the keywords PRIMARY KEY after a column in the table definition. You also can add a key definition as a separate item in the CREATE TABLE statement.

A primary key is specified using the keywords PRIMARY KEY followed by the name of the column in parentheses. You can also specify a UNIQUE KEY or UNIQUE INDEX, or simply a KEY or INDEX with no further constraints. The column name is given in parentheses after the key type.

The following statement shows an alternative CREATE TABLE statement for the products table in the sample database. The table it creates is the same as if PRIMARY KEY were specified alongside the product_code column and the name column was given the UNIQUE attribute.

```
CREATE TABLE products (
  product_code   VARCHAR(10),
  name           VARCHAR(40)    NOT NULL,
  weight         DECIMAL(6,2)   NOT NULL,
  price          DECIMAL(6,2)   NOT NULL,
  PRIMARY KEY (product_code),
  UNIQUE KEY (name)
)
```

You can use the ALTER TABLE command to add indexes to a table using this syntax in the same way you would add new columns to a table. The following example defines a new index on the customer_code column in the orders table:

```
mysql> ALTER TABLE orders
    -> ADD INDEX(customer_code);
Query OK, 10 rows affected (0.00 sec)
Records: 10  Duplicates: 0  Warnings: 0
```

Sample Index   Although it is not necessary for the sample tables that contain only very few rows, the previous example creates an index that would probably speed up database access on the orders table when it contains a large number of rows. The index could be used when you either query orders for a particular customer or join orders to the customers table.

Using CREATE INDEX

The CREATE INDEX command offers another way to add an index on a database column. This command requires you to name the index as well as specify the table name and column.

The following statement creates the same index you created in the previous example on orders.customer_code. The index is named cust_code_idx.

```
mysql> CREATE INDEX cust_code_idx
    -> ON orders(customer_code);
Query OK, 10 rows affected (0.01 sec)
Records: 10  Duplicates: 0  Warnings: 0
```

If you execute both this statement and the previous example, you will not see an error—MySQL will create two indexes on the same column of the same table. However, because each index name must be unique, you will generate an error if you try to execute this CREATE INDEX statement again.

Viewing Indexes on a Table

To view the keys or indexes on a table, use the SHOW KEYS or SHOW INDEXES commands. The result of both commands is the same; whether you use CREATE INDEX or define the column as a key makes no difference.

The following example shows the indexes on the orders table. The output shown assumes that you executed both of the previous two examples, so the index on customer_code was created twice.

```
mysql> SHOW INDEXES FROM orders;
+---------+------------+----------------+---------------+
| Table   | Non_unique | Key_name       | Column_name   |
+---------+------------+----------------+---------------+
| orders  |          0 | PRIMARY        | order_id      |
| orders  |          1 | customer_code  | customer_code |
| orders  |          1 | cust_code_idx  | customer_code |
+---------+------------+----------------+---------------+
3 rows in set (0.00 sec)
```

The output shown here has been modified because of space constraints in this book. The actual output you will see contains a few other columns.

The first row contains the primary key for the table. The other rows are the additional indexes you created. The one created through the ALTER TABLE statement was given the name customer_code, shown in the Key_name column. The Non_unique column contains 0 for the primary key and 1 for the other keys, which were not created with UNIQUE.

Duplicate Indexes   Although MySQL does not generate an error if you create the same index twice—as long as it does not have the same name—there is never a reason to do this. MySQL can use only one index, so the second simply takes up extra disk space. We drop one of the unnecessary indexes on this table in the next section.

Dropping Indexes

To drop an index from a table, you need to know its name, which you have to check using the SHOW INDEXES command unless you specified the name yourself.

The following command drops the `cust_code_idx` index using the `DROP INDEX` command, leaving all other indexes and all the data in the table intact:

```
mysql> DROP INDEX cust_code_idx
    -> ON orders;
Query OK, 10 rows affected (0.01 sec)
Records: 10  Duplicates: 0  Warnings: 0
```

Alternatively, you could use the `ALTER TABLE` command with `DROP INDEX`. The following statement would perform the same operation as the previous example:

```
ALTER TABLE orders DROP INDEX cust_code_idx;
```

Dropping a Primary Key   The only time you do not need to know the name of an index is when it is the primary key on the table. Then you can use `ALTER TABLE` *tablename* `DROP PRIMARY KEY`.

Partial Indexes

When creating an index on a string value, you can tell MySQL to use only part of the value rather than the whole string in the index. The following statement creates an index on the `name` column in the `customers` table, but using only the first five characters of the name:

```
ALTER TABLE customers
ADD INDEX (name(5));
```

Or, you can use the `CREATE INDEX` statement:

```
CREATE INDEX cust_name_idx
ON customers(name(5));
```

A partial index can be useful when you index columns that can potentially contain large values. The index will have a smaller storage requirement while still assisting queries in finding values from the column quickly.

MySQL compares the specified number of characters in the key to locate matching rows first. If more than one row matches the partial key, it checks those rows to find an exact match.

Compound Indexes

You can specify two or more columns when creating an index, and MySQL will create an index that uses the values from both columns in the order given. This is known as a compound index.

The following statement creates a compound index on the weight and price columns in the products table:

```
ALTER TABLE products
ADD INDEX (weight, price);
```

Or, you can use the CREATE INDEX statement:

```
CREATE INDEX products_weight_price_idx
ON products(weight, price);
```

Usually you create a compound index on two columns that are frequently used in a single query or are both used in a table join. MySQL can use only one index on each table in a query, so two separate indexes on the same two columns cannot both be used.

The index created by the previous example could speed up a query on the products table that had a filter on both weight and price. Additionally, because weight is the first column specified, this index could be used effectively on queries that filter just on weight. However, it would be ineffective on queries that filter on price only.

Compound Primary Keys   You can create a compound primary key by giving a comma-separated list of column names after the PRIMARY KEY keyword in the CREATE TABLE statement.

The Full-Text Index

The full-text index is a special type of index MySQL implements that is very efficient for free text searching. You can create a full-text index on a TEXT or VARCHAR type column and then perform text matching using the MATCH() function.

You specify a full-text index using the FULLTEXT keyword in the table definition or on an existing table using the ALTER TABLE statement. The following statement adds a full-text index to the customer_contacts table on the first_name and last_name columns:

```
mysql> ALTER TABLE customers
    -> ADD FULLTEXT(name);
Query OK, 6 rows affected (0.00 sec)
Records: 6  Duplicates: 0  Warnings: 0
```

The MATCH() function works only with columns that have a full-text index. You specify the column to search in parentheses—if you have more than one full-text index, you can specify a list of columns—followed by the keyword AGAINST and a list of values to search for.

The following example searches the customers table for a name that matches the string Corporation:

```
mysql> SELECT * FROM customers
    -> WHERE MATCH(name) AGAINST ('Corporation');
+---------------+---------------------+
| customer_code | name                |
+---------------+---------------------+
| SCICORP       | Science Corporation |
| CORPLTD       | Corporation Limited |
+---------------+---------------------+
2 rows in set (0.00 sec)
```

Full-Text Table Handlers   The full-text index feature is available only using the MyISAM storage engine. You cannot use FULLTEXT with an InnoDB table.

Foreign Key Constraints with InnoDB

The InnoDB table handler includes support for foreign key constraints, which are used to enforce the rule that a column value may contain only a value that is present in a given column in another table.

For example, a foreign key on the customer_code column in the orders table that references customers.customer_code would ensure that you can enter rows into orders only for customers that are already in the database.

The sample tables do not have their foreign keys enforced at the database level, to ensure that they work on systems on which InnoDB is not available. The following example shows how the CREATE TABLE statement for orders would be amended to include this constraint:

```
CREATE TABLE orders (
   order_id INT PRIMARY KEY AUTO_INCREMENT,
   customer_code VARCHAR(10) NOT NULL,
   order_date DATE NOT NULL,
   FOREIGN KEY (customer_code)
   REFERENCES customers(customer_code)
) ENGINE=InnoDB;
```

 Foreign Key Restrictions To create a foreign key constraint, both the table with the constraint and the table that it references must use the InnoDB storage engine. The previous example will fail if the customers table is a MyISAM table.

The following example attempts to insert a new row into the orders table and shows the error message that is displayed when the foreign key is violated:

```
mysql> INSERT INTO orders (customer_code, order_date)
    -> VALUES ('NODDY', NOW());
ERROR 1452 (23000): Cannot add or update a child row: a
Foreign key constraint fails (`mysql10/orders2`, CONSTRAINT
`orders2_ibfk_1` FOREIGN KEY (`customer_code`) REFERENCES
`customers` (`customer_code`))
```

Consider what might happen if you delete a record from the `customers` table for which there are corresponding rows in orders. The records in the orders table would then violate the foreign key constraint.

To avoid this, you can specify an action to take when values referenced by a foreign key are changed or removed using the `ON UPDATE` or `ON, DELETE` keywords in a `FOREIGN KEY` clause. The possible values are as follows:

- `CASCADE`—When a referenced value in the parent table is updated, corresponding rows in the child table have the same update performed on their foreign key columns. If the value in the parent table is deleted, rows in the child table are automatically deleted when a foreign key is deleted from the parent table.

- `SET NULL`—When a referenced value in the parent table is updated or deleted, corresponding rows in the child table have their foreign key columns set to `NULL`. This action is not possible if the foreign key column has the `NOT NULL` constraint.

- `NO ACTION`—Records will never be modified or deleted in the child table. Instead, if an `UPDATE` or `DELETE` on the parent table would change or remove a referenced value, the action is prohibited. This is the default action if no `ON UPDATE` or `ON DELETE` action is given.

The following statement can be used to add the foreign key described in the previous example to the `customers` table, using `CASCADE` for updates and `NO ACTION` to prevent referenced columns from being deleted from the parent table:

```
ALTER TABLE orders
ADD FOREIGN KEY(customer_code)
REFERENCES customers(customer_code)
ON UPDATE CASCADE
ON DELETE NO ACTION;
```

Then, if you update a record in the `customers` table, corresponding rows in orders will be updated with the same customer code.

```
mysql> UPDATE customers
    -> SET customer_code = 'NEWCODE'
    -> WHERE customer_code = 'MUSGRP';
```

```
Query OK, 1 row affected (0.01 sec)
Rows matched: 1  Changed: 1  Warnings: 0

mysql> SELECT * FROM orders
    -> WHERE customer_code = 'NEWCODE';
+----------+---------------+------------+
| order_id | customer_code | order_date |
+----------+---------------+------------+
|        6 | NEWCODE       | 2006-02-01 |
|        7 | NEWCODE       | 2006-02-02 |
|        9 | NEWCODE       | 2006-04-01 |
|       10 | NEWCODE       | 2006-04-01 |
+----------+---------------+------------+
4 rows in set (0.00 sec)
```

However, attempting to remove a referenced row from the customers
table is prohibited and gives an error, as shown in the following example:

```
mysql> DELETE FROM customers
    -> WHERE customer_code = 'SCICORP';
ERROR 1451 (23000): Cannot delete or update a parent row: a
foreign key constraint fails (`mysql10/orders`, CONSTRAINT
`orders_ibfk_1`FOREIGN KEY (`customer_code`) REFERENCES
`customers` (`customer_code`) ON DELETE NO ACTION ON UPDATE
CASCADE)
```

Referential Integrity The ON UPDATE and ON DELETE
actions of a foreign key constraint are essential for
maintaining referential integrity in your database.
Otherwise, you can end up with values in a foreign
key column that do not correspond to any record in
the parent table.

When you do not use database-level foreign key constraints, you must ensure that your application will
maintain referential integrity when updates or deletes
are performed on a referenced table.

Summary

In this lesson, you learned how indexes work in MySQL and how to add indexes to database columns. In the next lesson, you will learn how the MySQL privilege tables work and how to manage user access to a database.

LESSON 18
Managing User Access

In this lesson, you learn how to manage users and use the GRANT command to control their privileges on individual databases and tables.

Understanding MySQL Authentication

MySQL has a sophisticated multiuser access-control system that can allow or prevent each user from having access to a particular database or individual tables. You can even restrict the types of operations the user is able to perform on a table.

 Web Access When MySQL is used as the back end to a website, you will usually have only a single user account through which all the connections from the web scripts are performed. Your application will handle any additional user authentication that is required in the web browser.

Authenticating with MySQL

When you connect to a MySQL server, you provide a username and password to gain access. MySQL authenticates you using not only these login details, but also the hostname or IP address you are connecting from.

localhost   Often you communicate with MySQL only from localhost—that is, when you run the mysql client on the same machine as the MySQL server, or you access a database from an application or web script that is running on the same machine.

Not only do you need to supply a valid username and password for the database you want to gain access to, but you also need to satisfy MySQL that you are connecting from an allowed host for that user. If you try to connect with a username and password that are not valid for the host you are connecting from, access will be denied, even if the login information works from another host.

It is also possible for two users who have the same username but are connecting from two different hosts to use separate passwords and have separate privileges. Therefore, you should try to think of a MySQL user as a username plus a host when dealing with user permissions, rather than just the username. In other words, consider the access requirements for chris@localhost or chris@192.168.1.100, not for user chris.

MySQL Privileges

MySQL includes a number of individual privileges that determine the type of actions that a user can perform. For example, a user with the SELECT privilege may query a table, but the same user also requires the INSERT, DELETE, and UPDATE privileges to perform data manipulation on the same table.

A privilege can be granted to a user—remember, this means a user plus a host—at the table level. Therefore, two users with access to the same database can be given permission to use only the tables they require access to.

Table 18.1 lists the privileges that can be assigned. User permissions are set using the GRANT and REVOKE commands, which are discussed later in this chapter.

TABLE 18.1   Privileges in MySQL

ALTER	Allows use of ALTER TABLE.
ALTER ROUTINE	Alters or drops stored routines.
CREATE	Allows use of CREATE TABLE.
CREATE ROUTINE	Creates stored routines.
CREATE TEMPORARY TABLE	Allows use of CREATE TEMPORARY TABLE.
CREATE USER	Allows use of CREATE USER, DROP USER, RENAME USER, and REVOKE ALL PRIVILEGES.
CREATE VIEW	Allows use of CREATE VIEW.
DELETE	Allows use of DELETE.
DROP	Allows use of DROP TABLE.
EXECUTE	Allows the user to run stored routines.
FILE	Allows use of SELECT ... INTO OUTFILE and LOAD DATA INFILE.
INDEX	Allows use of CREATE INDEX and DROP INDEX.
INSERT	Allows use of INSERT.
LOCK TABLES	Allows use of LOCK TABLES on tables for which the user also has SELECT privileges.
PROCESS	Allows use of SHOW FULL PROCESSLIST.
RELOAD	Allows use of FLUSH.
REPLICATION CLIENT	Allows the user to ask where slave or master servers are.
REPLICATION SLAVE	Needed for replication slaves.
SELECT	Allows use of SELECT.

continues

TABLE 18.1   Continued

SHOW DATABASES	Allows use of SHOW DATABASES.
SHOW VIEW	Allows use of SHOW CREATE VIEW.
SHUTDOWN	Allows use of mysqladmin shutdown.
SUPER	Allows use of CHANGE MASTER, KILL, PURGE MASTER LOGS, and SET GLOBAL SQL statements. Allows mysqladmin debug command. Allows one extra connection to be made if maximum connections are reached.
UPDATE	Allows use of UPDATE.
USAGE	Allows connection without any specific privileges.

The MySQL Privilege Tables

Whether access is granted to MySQL is determined by data in the mysql database, which contains a number of tables that control user privileges.

Superuser   Access to the mysql database is usually available only to the MySQL root user. Only a MySQL superuser user should have access to the privilege tables.

Data from the user table is used for authentication. The Host, User, and Password columns contain the values used to validate a connection attempt. The Password column is encrypted, so you cannot view a user's actual password by querying this table.

The db database contains the default permissions that a user has for each database. The Db, User, and Host columns are followed by a series of privilege columns, such as Select_priv and Alter_priv. Those columns contain either a Y or an N value to indicate whether that privilege has been granted.

Individual table privileges are stored in the tables_priv table, using the Db, User, Host, and Table_name columns to identify the database table and user. The Table_priv column contains the name of the privilege granted. Whereas db contains one row per user and database, there is one row in tables_priv for each table-level privilege assigned.

Changing Privileges   Although it is possible to query and update the privilege tables directly, it is easier to use the commands described in the "User Management" section of this lesson to do so.

Furthermore, changes made to the privilege tables do not take effect until you issue the FLUSH PRIVILEGES command.

User Management

In this section, you learn how to manage user accounts and grant and revoke privileges.

Creating a User

Use the CREATE USER command to create a new user. The username given should be a username and a host, in the format *user@host*. Include the keywords IDENTIFIED BY to set a password for the new user.

Passwords   If you do not assign a password for a user, that user will be able to connect to MySQL without even supplying a password.

The following example creates a new user named chris that can connect only from localhost, with the password mypass:

```
mysql> CREATE USER chris@localhost IDENTIFIED BY 'mypass';
Query OK, 0 rows affected (0.02 sec)
```

You usually create new users when connected to MySQL as the root user, but if you want to allow other users to use the CREATE USER command, you should assign them the INSERT privilege on the mysql database. The underlying operation is an INSERT command that adds a record to mysql.user.

Setting or Changing a Password

The password values stored in the Password column of mysql.user are encrypted using a hashing algorithm that cannot be decoded back to the original password. You can perform the same hash using the PASSWORD() function.

You can use the SET PASSWORD command to reset a user's password, but you must use PASSWORD() to produce the encrypted password as part of this command. The following is an example:

```
mysql> SET PASSWORD FOR chris@localhost = PASSWORD('newpass');
Query OK, 0 rows affected (0.00 sec)
```

If you omit the PASSWORD() function, MySQL warns you that you did not supply a valid password.

```
mysql> SET PASSWORD FOR chris@localhost = 'newpass';
ERROR 1372 (HY000): Password hash should be a 41-digit
hexadecimal number
```

Any user can use SET PASSWORD, although only a superuser can change other users' passwords. To change the password for the logged-in user, omit the FOR *user* part, as follows:

```
mysql> SET PASSWORD = PASSWORD('newpass');
Query OK, 0 rows affected (0.00 sec)
```

Granting Privileges

To assign a privilege to a user, use the GRANT command. This can be done through an individual privilege, a list, or the ALL PRIVILEGES keyword, which allocates every privilege shown in Table 18.1 to the user.

The following example grants the SELECT and INSERT privileges on the products table in the mysql10 database to the new user chris@localhost:

```
mysql> GRANT SELECT, INSERT
    -> ON mysql10.products
    -> TO chris@localhost;
Query OK, 0 rows affected (0.00 sec)
```

If you connect as this user, the SHOW TABLES command reveals just one table; tables you do not have the SELECT privilege for are not displayed.

```
mysql> show tables;
+-------------------+
| Tables_in_mysql10 |
+-------------------+
| products          |
+-------------------+
1 row in set (0.00 sec)
```

You can query the products table and insert new rows, but if you attempt to use the DELETE command, permission will be denied.

```
mysql> INSERT INTO products
    -> (product_code, name, weight, price)
    -> VALUES
    -> ('MYPROD', 'My new product', 1.00, 1.99);
Query OK, 1 row affected (0.03 sec)
```

```
mysql> DELETE FROM products;
ERROR 1142 (42000): DELETE command denied to user
'chris'@'localhost' for table 'products'
```

Passing on Privileges

When you grant a privilege to a user, that user will be able to take advantage of the new access rights but cannot pass that privilege on to another user unless you specifically grant permission to do so.

To do this, use the keywords WITH GRANT OPTION in a GRANT statement. The following statement allows chris@localhost not only to query the products table, but also to use the GRANT command himself to give the SELECT privilege to other users:

```
mysql> GRANT SELECT
    -> ON mysql10.products
    -> TO chris@localhost
    -> WITH GRANT OPTION;
Query OK, 0 rows affected (0.00 sec)
```

Even though only the SELECT privilege is named in the previous statement, WITH GRANT OPTION allows this user to grant any privileges he possesses to another user.

Revoking Privileges

The opposite of granting a privilege is revoking, performed using the REVOKE command. Its syntax is similar to GRANT, as shown in the following example, which removes the INSERT privilege that was granted in the previous section.

```
mysql> REVOKE INSERT
    -> ON mysql10.products
    -> FROM chris@localhost;
Query OK, 0 rows affected (1.25 sec)
```

Only the INSERT privilege is revoked; the SELECT privilege that was assigned to this user at the same time as INSERT is unaffected.

Using Wildcards

You can grant privileges to usernames that match wildcard criteria by using the % and _ wildcard characters in the username.

You might actually want to create a user that can access the database from any remote host using the same username and password without needing to create a separate username for each possible host. Using % as the host part of the username accomplishes this, as shown in the following example:

```
mysql> CREATE USER 'chris@%' IDENTIFIED BY 'password';
Query OK, 0 rows affected (0.00 sec)

mysql> GRANT SELECT, INSERT
    -> ON mysql10.products
    -> TO 'chris@%';
Query OK, 0 rows affected (0.00 sec)
```

Wildcard Usernames The username in a CREATE USER, GRANT, or REVOKE command must be enclosed in quotes if it contains a wildcard character. Otherwise, MySQL gives an error.

If you want to grant access only to a user from a particular range of IP addresses, you could use a statement like the following:

```
mysql> CREATE USER 'localuser@192.168.1.1_'
    -> IDENTIFIED BY 'localpass';
Query OK, 0 rows affected (0.00 sec)
```

In this case, the user would be authenticated only if connecting from an IP address in the range 192.168.1.10 to 192.168.1.19.

Viewing a User's Privileges

You can see what privileges have been granted to a user with the SHOW GRANTS command. The output from the command is a list of GRANT statements that can be used to re-create the user with the same set of privileges.

The following example shows the privileges for chris@localhost that were set up throughout this lesson.

```
mysql> SHOW GRANTS FOR chris@localhost;
+----------------------------------------------------------------+
| Grants for chris@localhost___                                  |
+----------------------------------------------------------------+
| GRANT USAGE ON *.* TO 'chris'@'localhost' IDENTIFIED          |
| BY PASSWORD '*D8DECEC305209EEFEC43008E1D420E1AA06B19E0'        |
| GRANT SELECT ON `mysql10`.`products` TO 'chris'@'localhost'   |
+----------------------------------------------------------------+
2 rows in set (0.04 sec)
```

Notice that this output does not contain each GRANT statement issued for the user, and does not contain any REVOKE statements. After revoking INSERT, the user has only the SELECT privilege.

Deleting a User

To completely remove a user, in MySQL 5.0.2 and above you can use the
DROP USER command, as shown:

```
mysql> DROP USER chris@localhost;
Query OK, 0 rows affected (0.00 sec)
```

In earlier versions of MySQL, you must revoke the user's privileges first
and then manually delete the appropriate record from the mysql.user
table. The following example shows the steps required to reproduce the
previous DROP USER command:

```
mysql> REVOKE ALL PRIVILEGES
    -> ON *.*
    -> FROM chris@localhost;
Query OK, 0 rows affected (0.01 sec)

mysql> DELETE FROM mysql.user
    -> WHERE User = 'chris'
    -> AND Host = 'localhost';
Query OK, 1 row affected (0.00 sec)

mysql> FLUSH PRIVILEGES;
Query OK, 0 rows affected (0.01 sec)
```

> **Dropping Users**   To use the DROP USER command, you
> must have the CREATE USER privilege if you are not a
> MySQL superuser. To delete the user using the manual
> method, however, you must have the DELETE privilege
> for the mysql.user table.

Summary

In this lesson, you learned how to manage users and control their access
to MySQL databases using the privilege system. In the next section of the
book, you will learn how to use some of the new features of MySQL 5.0.

LESSON 19
Views

In this lesson, you learn how to use views to create pseudo-tables based on other tables in your database. Views are available in MySQL in version 5.0.1 and higher.

Understanding Views

A view is a pseudo-table. In SQL, you can reference a view just like you reference a table in a SELECT statement. You can also use some views with INSERT, UPDATE, and DELETE statements.

Views are a tool of convenience. For example, if you find yourself frequently performing the same join, you might find it more convenient to create a view to use in your queries instead.

Creating a View

You create a view with the CREATE VIEW command. The following example creates a simple view—every column from the customer_contacts table is included, but a WHERE clause restricts the rows returned to only those with the given customer_code.

```
mysql> CREATE VIEW custview AS
    -> SELECT * FROM customer_contacts
    -> WHERE customer_code = 'SCICORP';
Query OK, 0 rows affected (0.04 sec)
```

The command executes silently if there is no error. An error in the SELECT statement of a CREATE VIEW command produces the same error you would get if you had executed the query directly.

After you have created a view, you can perform a SELECT statement using it, as follows:

```
mysql> SELECT first_name, last_name
    -> FROM custview
    -> ORDER BY last_name;
+------------+-----------+
| first_name | last_name |
+------------+-----------+
| Marie      | Curie     |
| Charles    | Darwin    |
| Albert     | Einstein  |
| Benjamin   | Franklin  |
+------------+-----------+
4 rows in set (0.01 sec)
```

The output contains only the rows that were filtered in the CREATE VIEW statement. Other rows from the customer_contacts table cannot be accessed using this view.

 Views Are Not Tables   It is important to understand that the previous statement does not create a copy of the customer_contacts table using a snapshot of the data. Whenever a view is accessed, the underlying query is executed to generate the values in the pseudo-table.

Therefore, if new records are inserted into customer_contacts for this customer, they will also appear in custview.

The following example creates a view that includes a table join on the customers and customer_contacts table. This time, the CREATE VIEW statement also specifies a list of columns and includes an expression.

```
mysql> CREATE VIEW customer_details AS
    -> SELECT customers.customer_code, name, email,
    ->           concat(last_name, ', ', first_name) AS full_name
    -> FROM customers, customer_contacts
    -> WHERE customers.customer_code =
customer_contacts.customer_code;
Query OK, 0 rows affected (0.00 sec)
```

An alias is required for the CONCAT() expression, to give that column a name in the view. Showing the columns in this view reveals that there is indeed a column named full_name:

```
mysql> DESCRIBE customer_details;
+---------------+-------------+------+-----+---------+-------+
| Field         | Type        | Null | Key | Default | Extra |
+---------------+-------------+------+-----+---------+-------+
| customer_code | varchar(10) | NO   |     |         |       |
| name          | varchar(40) | NO   |     |         |       |
| email         | text        | YES  |     | NULL    |       |
| full_name     | varchar(62) | NO   |     |         |       |
+---------------+-------------+------+-----+---------+-------+
4 rows in set (0.00 sec)
```

Column Aliases Where you use a derived column in a view, you must give the column an alias; otherwise, you will not be able to select its values by name. The name assigned if you do not give an alias will be based on the expression used to calculate the column.

You must also use aliases if the SELECT statement in a view will return two columns with the same name. MySQL returns an error if the column names in a view are not unique.

Go ahead and select values from this column—you will see that the concatenated full name is returned for each value in the table.

```
mysql> SELECT full_name
    -> FROM customer_details;
+--------------------+
| full_name          |
+--------------------+
| Lincoln, Abraham   |
| Nixon, Richard     |
...
| Britten, Benjamin  |
| Lennon, John       |
+--------------------+
11 rows in set (0.00 sec)
```

> **View Naming** The name of a view must be unique across both views and tables. A view cannot have the same name as a table in the same database.

Privileges and Views

To create views, you must have the CREATE VIEW privilege. This is a separate privilege from CREATE, which enables you to create tables and indexes. If a user account was granted ALL PRIVILEGES, it includes CREATE VIEW.

To assign the CREATE VIEW privilege to a user, use a statement like the following:

```
mysql> GRANT CREATE VIEW ON mysql10.* TO chris@localhost;
Query OK, 0 rows affected (0.00 sec)
```

> **Using Views** If you have upgraded to MySQL 5.0.1 or higher from an earlier version, you will need to upgrade the grant tables using the mysql_fix privilege_tables command to assign the CREATE VIEW privilege. Refer to the release notes with your version of MySQL for more information.

You must also have the SELECT privilege on all the tables that are referenced in the SELECT statement of a CREATE VIEW statement. If you cannot query the tables yourself, you cannot create a new view that uses them.

You can, however, grant the SELECT privilege on a view you created to another user without giving that user the SELECT privilege on each table in the view. For instance, a system user could have access to the customer_details view without being able to query either customers or 190customer_contacts directly.

Updating Views

Some views are updateable, but you cannot always use a view in an UPDATE, INSERT, or DELETE statement. Several features of the underlying query that would cause a view to be nonupdateable.

If the view contains a join, you can usually perform a SELECT only on the view. MySQL cannot insert into two tables simultaneously, even with the relationship between the tables specified in the join condition.

You can insert into a view that uses a join only if it is an inner-join and also only if all the columns you insert into are from the same table.

You cannot insert into any view that uses the UNION or UNION ALL operator.

A view cannot be updated, even if it is based on only one table, if its query contains any of the following features:

- The DISTINCT keyword
- A GROUP BY clause
- Any aggregate function, such as SUM()
- A column derived from any function, expression, or subquery
- A correlated subquery in the WHERE clause
- The view's algorithm is TEMPTABLE—see the section "View Algorithms" later in this lesson for more information.

 Cascaded Views   It follows that if a view selects data from another nonupdateable view. It, too, will be nonupdateable.

Finding Information About Views

You can use the SHOW CREATE VIEW command to see the underlying query text for a view. The output might not be the query you entered verbatim—for example, a SELECT * will be expanded to select the individual fields, and several optional attributes of the CREATE VIEW command will be present. Any formatting you used when entering the CREATE VIEW statement will be lost.

The output of SHOW CREATE VIEW is designed to give you a single command that can be run on any MySQL server to reproduce that view. The following shows this for the customer_details view:

```
mysql> SHOW CREATE VIEW customer_details
    -> \G
*************************** 1. row ***************************
View: customer_details
Create View: CREATE ALGORITHM=UNDEFINED DEFINER=
`root`@`localhost` SQL SECURITY DEFINER VIEW
`customer_details` AS select `customers`.
`customer_code` AS `customer_code`,`customers`.
`name` AS `name`,`customer_contacts`.`email` AS
`email`,concat(`customer_contacts`.`last_name`,
_latin1', ', `customer_contacts`.`first_name`)
AS `concat(last_name, ', ', first_name)` from
(`customers` join `customer_contacts`)
where (`customers`.`customer_code` =
`customer_contacts`.`customer_code`)
1 row in set (0.00 sec)
```

Show Create View Output   In some versions of MySQL, the column headings in the output from SHOW CREATE VIEW were labeled Table and Create Table so don't be confused if you see this instead. The headings were changed to View and Create View in MySQL 5.0.11.

Showing Views   Because views behave just like tables, the SHOW TABLES command will show all your views as well as your tables.

View Algorithms

The output from the previous example included an optional attribute in the `CREATE VIEW` statement: `ALGORITHM=UNDEFINED`. This attribute is a MySQL-specific extension to the SQL language used to instruct MySQL on how to process a view. When this is `UNDEFINED`—which will be the case unless you explicitly give an algorithm—MySQL chooses the algorithm.

The `MERGE` algorithm is usually the most efficient way for a view to be processed. The underlying SQL is merged into the SQL statement, and the query is executed in one go. Consider the following query using the `custview` view:

```
SELECT first_name, last_name
FROM custview
ORDER BY last_name;
```

If the `custview` view is executed using the `MERGE` algorithm, the query is actually executed as if you entered the following:

```
SELECT first_name, last_name
FROM (SELECT * FROM customer_contacts
      WHERE customer_code = 'SCICORP')
ORDER BY last_name
```

However, if `custview` uses the `TEMPTABLE` algorithm, the process would be as if you had executed the following steps:

```
CREATE TEMPORARY TABLE tempview AS
SELECT * FROM customer_contacts
WHERE customer_code = 'SCICORP';

SELCET first_name, last_name
FROM tempview
ORDER BY last_name;

DROP TEMPORARY TABLE tempview;
```

The `TEMPTABLE` algorithm must be used if the query contains an aggregate function, a `GROUP BY` clause, the `DISTINCT` keyword, or a `UNION`.

Altering and Dropping Views

To change the definition of a view, use the ALTER VIEW command. The syntax is just the same as CREATE VIEW, but the existing view is replaced with the new definition. The following example changes the definition of custview to use a different customer_code in the filter:

```
mysql> ALTER VIEW custview AS
    -> SELECT * FROM customer_contacts
    -> WHERE customer_code = 'MUSGRP';
Query OK, 0 rows affected (0.00 sec)
```

To drop a view, simply use DROP VIEW as follows:

```
mysql> DROP VIEW custview;
Query OK, 0 rows affected (0.00 sec)
```

Summary

In this lesson, you learned how to use views as pseudo-tables in MySQL. In the next lesson, you will learn about stored procedures.

LESSON 20
Stored Routines

In this lesson, you learn how to create and execute database-level stored routines. Stored procedures and functions are available in MySQL 5.0.1 and higher.

Understanding Stored Routines

A stored procedure is a series of SQL statements stored in a MySQL database. For a frequently executed series of commands, this is a time-saving feature—you only need to execute the stored procedure.

A stored function is a stored routine that can return a value to SQL. A useful feature is the capability to define libraries of functions so that you can perform an operation on your database from any client program. Libraries of commonly used functions and procedures help reduce code duplication and make your systems easier to maintain.

 Function Libraries If you use multiple APIs to communicate with your database, you can execute the same function from each language without having to rewrite the function.

Creating a Stored Procedure

To create a new stored procedure, use the CREATE PROCEDURE command, followed by a procedure name and a list of SQL statements that form the procedure body.

The following is a very simple example. The procedure created, named yesterday, takes no arguments; it simply selects and displays the date and time precisely 1 day ago.

```
mysql> CREATE PROCEDURE yesterday()
    -> SELECT DATE_ADD(NOW(), INTERVAL -1 DAY) as yesterday;
Query OK, 0 rows affected (0.01 sec)
```

To execute a procedure, use the CALL command. The following shows typical output from the yesterday procedure:

```
mysql> CALL yesterday();
+---------------------+
| yesterday           |
+---------------------+
| 2006-02-07 03:02:21 |
+---------------------+
1 row in set (0.00 sec)
```

Note that both the procedure definition and the CALL command include a set of parentheses after the name of the procedure. The parentheses are used to pass optional arguments to a procedure, but they must be included even if no arguments are required.

The following example creates a new procedure named longdate that displays a given date value in a predefined format:

```
mysql> CREATE PROCEDURE longdate (IN date DATE) as long_date
    -> SELECT DATE_FORMAT(date, '%W %D %M %Y');
Query OK, 0 rows affected (0.00 sec)
```

When you call this procedure, you must supply a date argument in the parentheses, as in the following example:

```
mysql> CALL longdate('2006-05-03');
+-----------------------+
| long_date             |
+-----------------------+
| Wednesday 3rd May 2006 |
+-----------------------+
1 row in set (0.00 sec)
```

Note that procedures do not return a value; to do that, you must use a function. Therefore, you cannot nest these two procedures (for example, to use yesterday as an argument to longdate). Both functions simply perform a SELECT statement, and their output is displayed in the mysql monitor.

The real power of stored routines lies in their capability to execute many different SQL commands in a single procedure call. When a procedure contains more than one SQL statement, you must use the BEGIN and END keywords around the procedure body.

The following example is a procedure that applies a given percentage increase to all the prices in the products table, and then displays the new average price for all products:

```
CREATE PROCEDURE price_hike (increase FLOAT)
BEGIN
  UPDATE products
  SET price = price * (1+(increase/100));

  SELECT CONCAT('Average price is now ',
                AVG(price)) as new_price
  FROM products;
END
```

Before you attempt to create this procedure in MySQL, consider that the semicolon characters within the procedure are intended only to terminate the individual SQL statements, not the CREATE PROCEDURE command. This creates a conflict that must be worked around.

To keep the mysql program from treating the semicolons within a function as terminators for the CREATE PROCEDURE command, you must define a new terminator character using the delimiter, or \d, command.

 Delimiter Characters The delimiter can be any character or series of characters you choose, but you must make sure that it will not otherwise appear in the body of the CREATE PROCEDURE statement.

The following example sets the delimiter to // before creating the new procedure:

```
mysql> delimiter //
mysql> CREATE PROCEDURE price_hike (increase FLOAT)
    -> BEGIN
    ->    UPDATE products
    ->    SET price = price * (1+(increase/100));
    ->
    ->    SELECT CONCAT('Average price is now ',
    ->                    AVG(price)) as new_price
    ->    FROM products;
    -> END
    -> //
Query OK, 0 rows affected (0.00 sec)
```

Using Delimiters   Bear in mind that after the delimiter has been redefined, you must use that character until you specify a new delimiter or begin a new mysql session.

Unless otherwise specified, the following examples in this lesson assume that ; is the current statement-terminator character.

Creating a Stored Function

To create a new stored function, use the CREATE FUNCTION command. You must provide a function name, a list of arguments, and the return value data type before giving the list of SQL statements that form the function body.

The following example shows how the yesterday procedure from the previous section can be implemented as a function:

```
mysql> CREATE FUNCTION yesterday()
    -> RETURNS DATE
    -> RETURN date_add(NOW(), interval -1 day);
Query OK, 0 rows affected (0.00 sec)
```

Functions always return a value, so you must always give a return data type. The RETURN keyword is used to prefix a value or expression for the return value.

The return type for this function is set as DATE, so any SQL statement that calls the function will treat its result as a date value. Therefore, you can use the result from the yesterday() function as an argument to the longdate procedure.

```
mysql> CALL longdate(yesterday());
+---------------------------+
| long_date                 |
+---------------------------+
| Tuesday 7th February 2006 |
+---------------------------+
1 row in set (0.01 sec)
```

 Routine Names   Each procedure name must be unique, as must each function name. However, it is possible for a function and a procedure to share the same name: The yesterday() function was successfully created without dropping the yesterday procedure.

Because functions are called from SQL statements and procedures are called using CALL, this never presents a conflict in your code. However, you should consider using unique names for all stored routines, to avoid confusion.

Most functions require an argument, specified in parentheses after the function name in the CREATE FUNCTION statement.

Only IN arguments are possible with a function—data is naturally passed out of the function via the return value—so the IN keyword is not required in the argument list.

The following example creates a function named order_total() that takes an order_id argument and returns the total value of the items that make up that order:

```
mysql> delimiter //
mysql> CREATE FUNCTION order_total(id INT)
    -> RETURNS DECIMAL(7,2)
    -> BEGIN
```

```
    ->    DECLARE total_price DECIMAL(7,2);
    ->
    ->    SELECT SUM(ol.quantity * p.price) INTO total_price
    ->    FROM   order_lines ol, products p
    ->    WHERE  ol.product_code = p.product_code
    ->    AND    ol.order_id = id;
    ->
    ->    RETURN total_price;
    -> END
    -> //
Query OK, 0 rows affected (0.00 sec)
```

You can then call order_total with a valid order_id value, as follows:

```
mysql> SELECT order_total(5);
+-----------------+
| order_total(5) |
+-----------------+
|          259.80 |
+-----------------+
1 row in set (0.00 sec)
```

Using Variables

The DECLARE instruction in the order_total() function declares a variable named total_price, defined as type INT.

You can use variables to store the result from a SQL query—in order_total(), the result of the query was assigned by a query using SELECT ... INTO—or by using SET to assign a value to a variable.

Variables declared within a stored routine have local scope only and cannot be referenced outside the particular procedure or function in which they exist. In order_total(), the variable was required only to return the result of the query from the function.

MySQL also supports session variables, which have global scope for the duration of the current MySQL connection. Session variables do not need to be declared; their names are simply prefixed with the @ symbol whenever they are required.

The following example creates a procedure named store_time that assigns the current time into the session variable @time:

```
mysql> CREATE PROCEDURE store_time()
    -> SET @time=NOW();
Query OK, 0 rows affected (0.00 sec)
```

After you have called store_time in a MySQL session, you can use @time in any SQL statement to reference this value. This variable retains the time that the store_time procedure was last called:

```
mysql> CALL store_time();
Query OK, 0 rows affected (0.00 sec)
```

```
mysql> SELECT @time;
+---------------------+
| @time               |
+---------------------+
| 2006-02-08 20:25:12 |
+---------------------+
1 row in set (0.00 sec)
```

If you disconnect from MySQL and reconnect, the values of any session variables you have set up are lost. The value of @time will be NULL if you have not called store_time in the current session.

Getting Information About Stored Routines

To view the stored procedures and functions in a database, use the SHOW PROCEDURE STATUS and SHOW FUNCTION STATUS commands, respectively. The following example output (in long query format) shows the two sample functions created in the previous section:

```
mysql> SHOW FUNCTION STATUS\G
********** 1. row **********
            Db: mysql10
          Name: order_total
          Type: FUNCTION
       Definer: root@localhost
      Modified: 2006-02-08 17:11:20
       Created: 2006-02-08 17:11:20
 Security_type: DEFINER
       Comment:
********** 2. row **********
            Db: mysql10
          Name: yesterday
          Type: FUNCTION
```

```
    Definer: root@localhost
    Modified: 2006-02-08 17:14:47
     Created: 2006-02-08 17:14:47
Security_type: DEFINER
     Comment:
2 rows in set (0.00 sec)
```

Database-Level Routines Stored routines exist at the database level, and each routine is associated with a particular database on the MySQL server.

You can call a procedure or function from a database other than the current one by prefixing the routine name with the database name. Any SQL executed by the routine will be performed on the database to which that routine belongs.

To view the body of a procedure or function, use the SHOW CREATE PROCEDURE and SHOW CREATE FUNCTION commands. The following shows a sample output:

```
mysql> SHOW CREATE FUNCTION order_total \G
*************************** 1. row ***************************
       Function: order_total
       sql_mode:
Create Function: CREATE FUNCTION `order_total`(id INT)
RETURNS decimal(7,2)
BEGIN
    DECLARE total_price DECIMAL(7,2);
    SELECT SUM(ol.quantity * p.price) INTO total_price
    FROM  order_lines ol, products p
    WHERE ol.product_code = p.product_code
    AND   ol.order_id = id;

    RETURN total_price;
    END
1 row in set (0.00 sec)
```

Dropping a Stored Routine

To drop a stored routine from the database, use the DROP PROCEDURE and DROP FUNCTION commands. As with other DROP commands, you can include the IF EXISTS keywords to avoid an error if you attempt to drop a function that does not exist.

The following statement drops the yesterday procedure, if it exists:

```
mysql> DROP PROCEDURE IF EXISTS yesterday;
Query OK, 1 rows affected (0.00 sec)
```

Privileges and Stored Routines

Stored procedures require the presence of the proc table in the mysql database. This system table is created during installation of MySQL 5.0. If you upgrade from an earlier version of MySQL, you must update the grant tables using the mysql_fix_privilege_tables script.

To create a new routine, a user needs the CREATE ROUTINE privilege. To modify or delete a routine, a user must have the ALTER ROUTINE privilege. These privileges always apply to both procedures and functions.

A user must have the EXECUTE privilege to execute a stored procedure. As the creator of a stored routine, you have this privilege automatically. However, you grant other users access to your routine manually.

You must indicate in the GRANT command whether the routine is a procedure or a function. The following statement allows the user chris@localhost to execute the order_total() function:

```
mysql> GRANT EXECUTE ON FUNCTION order_total
    -> TO chris@localhost;
Query OK, 0 rows affected (0.00 sec)
```

Summary

In this lesson, you learned how to use stored routines in MySQL. In the next lesson, you will learn how to use triggers to execute SQL procedures automatically when certain database events take place.

LESSON 21
Triggers

In this lesson, you learn how to create triggers that can perform predefined SQL operations automatically when database-level events occur.

Understanding Triggers

A trigger is a stored database object that contains a series of SQL commands, set to activate automatically when certain events take place.

Each trigger is associated with a table. You can create a trigger that will fire when an INSERT, UPDATE, or DELETE takes place on the named table.

REPLACE Remember that when you use a REPLACE statement, MySQL actually performs a DELETE followed by an INSERT. Therefore, the REPLACE command will activate a DELETE trigger if the row already exists and will always activate an INSERT trigger.

Using Triggers

Triggers are used to perform more database operations when a certain type of database operation is initiated. You can use this property of triggers to perform automatic maintenance on your data or to monitor changes that have been made for audit purposes.

To create a new trigger, use the CREATE TRIGGER statement. You must give the trigger a unique name and then provide the timing, action, and table that will cause the trigger to fire. For example, to create a trigger that will fire every time a row is deleted from the products table, you would construct a trigger as follows:

```
CREATE TRIGGER trigger_name
BEFORE DELETE ON products
FOR EACH ROW
BEGIN
  ...
END
```

The timing for a trigger can be BEFORE or AFTER, indicating whether the trigger code should be executed immediately before or immediately after the SQL statement that causes the trigger to fire.

The keywords FOR EACH ROW are part of the CREATE TRIGGER syntax and are required in every trigger.

If the trigger body contains more than one line of code, you must enclose the SQL statements with the BEGIN and END keywords. As with stored routines, you also need to redefine the delimiter character if the trigger body contains multiple statements—refer to Lesson 20, "Stored Routines," for more information.

When a trigger is activated, the stored code can access the data record that caused the trigger event to occur. You can reference two pseudotables in the trigger body. Use OLD to reference deleted values and the previous values from an updated row. Use NEW to reference the new values in the database when using UPDATE or INSERT.

Creating an Audit Trail

A common use for triggers is to create a full audit trail on critical data tables. MySQL can do much of the hard work for you so you don't have to build this feature into your application.

This example creates an audit trail on the products table. First, however, a new audit table must be created to record the changes as they are made. The table should be created using the following statement:

```
CREATE TABLE products_audit (
  audit_date    TIMESTAMP,
  audit_user    VARCHAR(40)    NOT NULL,
  audit_action  ENUM('update','delete'),
  product_code  VARCHAR(10)    NOT NULL,
  name          VARCHAR(40)    NOT NULL,
```

```
    weight          DECIMAL(6,2)    NOT NULL,
    price           DECIMAL(6,2)    NOT NULL
);
```

Two triggers are required to log both DELETE and UPDATE actions on the products table. Each trigger will store a copy of the previous record to the audit table, along with the date and time and the user who issued the SQL command.

The DELETE trigger is created using the following statement:

```
mysql> CREATE TRIGGER products_delete_trigger
    -> BEFORE DELETE ON products
    -> FOR EACH ROW
    -> INSERT INTO products_audit
    ->     (audit_user, audit_action,
    ->      product_code, name, weight, price)
    -> VALUES (CURRENT_USER(), 'delete',
    ->     OLD.product_code, OLD.name, OLD.weight, OLD.price);
Query OK, 0 rows affected (0.00 sec)
```

The trigger will fire whenever a row is deleted from products, and it will take place immediately before that row is actually deleted. The OLD pseudotable allows the trigger code to access the old values before they are deleted.

If you delete the MIDI product from the database, a new record will be created in the audit table containing its former values.

```
mysql> DELETE FROM products
    -> WHERE product_code = 'MIDI';
Query OK, 1 row affected (0.00 sec)

mysql> SELECT * FROM products_audit \G
*************************** 1. row ***************************
  audit_date: 2006-02-08 22:12:54
  audit_user: chris@localhost
audit_action: delete
product_code: MIDI
        name: Medium product
      weight: 4.50
       price: 9.99
1 row in set (0.00 sec)
```

The UPDATE trigger works in a very similar way:

```
mysql> CREATE TRIGGER products_update_trigger
    -> BEFORE UPDATE ON products
    -> FOR EACH ROW
    -> INSERT INTO products_audit
    ->     (audit_user, audit_action,
    ->        product_code, name, weight, price)
    -> VALUES (CURRENT_USER(), 'update',
    ->        OLD.product_code, OLD.name, OLD.weight, OLD.price);
Query OK, 0 rows affected (0.00 sec)
```

Creating a Data-Maintenance Trigger

Triggers also can maintain values in other areas of your database, based on certain database events. The following example demonstrates this principle.

This trigger implements a dynamic pricing system for the products table, based on supply and demand. The rules for this example are fairly crude: Whenever an order is placed for a product, increase its price by 1% for each unit ordered and decrease the price of the least popular product by the same amount. Of course, you will need to make sure that this rule will not cause a product's price to drop to 0 or become negative.

The steps to implementing this trigger are as follows:

1. Whenever a new record is inserted into order_lines, calculate 1% of the price multiplied by the quantity sold.

2. Add this amount to the product that was ordered.

3. Find the product with the fewest sales and reduce its price by the same amount.

The CREATE TRIGGER statement is shown here in full:

```
mysql> delimiter //
mysql> CREATE TRIGGER supply_and_demand
    ->    AFTER INSERT ON order_lines
    ->    FOR EACH ROW
    -> BEGIN
    ->    DECLARE price_increase DECIMAL(7,2);
    ->
```

```
->    SELECT ROUND(price * 0.01 * NEW.quantity, 2)
->    INTO price_increase
->    FROM products
->    WHERE product_code = NEW.product_code;
->
->    UPDATE products
->    SET price = price + price_increase
->    WHERE product_code = NEW.product_code;
->
->    UPDATE products
->    SET price = GREATEST(1.00, price - price_increase)
->    WHERE product_code = (
->      SELECT product_code
->      FROM order_lines
->      WHERE product_code != NEW.product_code
->      GROUP BY product_code
->      ORDER BY SUM(quantity)
->      LIMIT 1
->    );
->
-> END
-> //
Query OK, 0 rows affected (0.00 sec)
```

Let's take this trigger a step at a time. The trigger is set to fire AFTER
INSERT on the order_lines table—this is the table that contains details on
how many of each product form part of an order.

The first line of the trigger code declares a local variable named
price_increase that will be used to store the amount by which the product sold will be increased and the least popular product will be decreased.

The next step is done in the following statement:

```
SELECT ROUND(price * 0.01 * NEW.quantity, 2)
INTO price_increase
FROM products
WHERE product_code = NEW.product_code;
```

The value of price_increase is calculated from the price of the product
that has been sold and the quantity in this order. Note that the NEW
pseudotable contains only the columns from order_lines—the table that
causes the trigger to fire when an INSERT is performed—so you have to
query the products table using NEW.product_code to find that product's
price.

The next step performs a straightforward update on the products table, increasing the price for NEW.product by price_increase.

Finally, the price of the least popular product is decreased using the following statement:

```
UPDATE products
SET price = GREATEST(1.00, price - price_increase)
WHERE product_code = (
  SELECT product_code
  FROM order_lines
  WHERE product_code != NEW.product_code
  GROUP BY product_code
  ORDER BY SUM(quantity)
  LIMIT 1
);
```

The GREATEST function ensures that the lowest a price can go when decreased is $1. The price value is set for the product_code returned by the subquery. Grouping by product_code and ordering by SUM(quantity)—the total number of units ordered for each product—the subquery will return products with those that have the fewest number of orders first.

The output from the following query shows the popularity of the products based on the initial values in order_lines from the sample database:

```
mysql> SELECT product_code, SUM(quantity)
    -> FROM order_lines
    -> GROUP BY product_code
    -> ORDER BY SUM(quantity)
    -> ;
+--------------+---------------+
| product_code | SUM(quantity) |
+--------------+---------------+
| MIDI         |            10 |
| MINI         |            36 |
| MAXI         |            48 |
+--------------+---------------+
3 rows in set (0.00 sec)
```

The following query shows the initial products and their prices from the sample database:

```
mysql> SELECT * FROM products;
+--------------+-----------------+--------+-------+
| product_code | name            | weight | price |
+--------------+-----------------+--------+-------+
| MINI         | Small product   |   1.50 |  5.99 |
| MIDI         | Medium product  |   4.50 |  9.99 |
| MAXI         | Large product   |   8.00 | 15.99 |
+--------------+-----------------+--------+-------+
3 rows in set (0.00 sec)
```

To test this trigger, let's create a new order line for an existing order:

```
mysql> INSERT INTO order_lines
    -> (order_id, product_code, quantity)
    -> VALUES (1, 'MIDI', 10);
Query OK, 1 row affected (0.00 sec)
```

When the products table is queried, you can see that the prices have been adjusted accordingly:

```
+--------------+-----------------+--------+-------+
| product_code | name            | weight | price |
+--------------+-----------------+--------+-------+
| MINI         | Small product   |   1.50 |  4.99 |
| MIDI         | Medium product  |   4.50 | 10.99 |
| MAXI         | Large product   |   8.00 | 15.99 |
+--------------+-----------------+--------+-------+
3 rows in set (0.00 sec)
```

The price of the product ordered (MIDI) has gone up by $1. One percent of its original value is $0.10, and the quantity ordered is 10. The MINI product has been decreased in price by the same $1.

Getting Information About Triggers

To see the triggers on a database, use the SHOW TRIGGERS command. The output contains a list of all the triggers that have been created. The Timing and Event columns show when the trigger will fire, and the Table column contains the associated table name.

A lot of output is produced because the output also contains the entire trigger body code. To view only the triggers for a particular table, use SHOW TRIGGERS LIKE 'table_name'.

Dropping Triggers

A trigger remains always active while it exists in the database. To remove a trigger, you must use the DROP TRIGGER command along with the name you gave to the trigger when you created it.

 Disabling Triggers If you want to disable a trigger but think you might need to reactivate it later, you still have to drop the trigger from the database. Be sure to take a copy of the CREATE TRIGGER statement from the output of SHOW TRIGGERS first.

The following example drops the supply_and_demand trigger:

```
mysql> DROP TRIGGER supply_and_demand;
Query OK, 0 rows affected (0.00 sec)
```

Privileges and Triggers

A user must have the SUPER privilege to use the CREATE TRIGGER command; no separate privilege exists to allow users to create triggers.

Although this means that all triggers are created and owned by a MySQL superuser, a user who issues a SQL statement that causes a trigger to fire still requires sufficient privileges to execute the trigger code.

Summary

In this lesson, you learned how to use database triggers in MySQL. In the next part of this book, you will learn how to interface with a MySQL database using various programming languages.

LESSON 22
Using ODBC

In this lesson, you learn how to use MySQL as the database back end to another application using ODBC.

Understanding ODBC

ODBC stands for Open Database Connectivity, a standard interface for accessing SQL-based databases. ODBC enables you to implement database independence in an application because any database server that speaks ODBC would respond to the communication from the client in exactly the same way.

You can also use ODBC to connect a database server to a client where there is otherwise no support available. So if MySQL does not include a specific API, you can still use it as your database back end through ODBC.

Obtaining MyODBC

The ODBC driver for MySQL is called Connector/ODBC and is available as a separate package, downloadable from http://dev.mysql.com/downloads/. The current stable version is 3.51, which implements the ODBC 3.51 specification.

 MyODBC Historically, the ODBC driver for MySQL was called MyODBC, so you might see it called by this name. The new name is consistent with other MySQL data drivers, including Connector/J for Java and Connector/Net for .NET.

Connecting to MyODBC

To communicate with a database, you need to specify a *data source*, which is exactly what it says—a source from which data can be fetched using an ODBC connection.

Each data source needs to be defined only once and is given a unique name known as a *Data Source Name*, or DSN. The DSN contains the connection parameters that identify a MySQL server and the user authentication required to log on.

Creating a Data Source on Windows

From the Start menu, select Settings, Control Panel, and then open Administrative Tools. Double-click Data Sources (ODBC)—on older versions of Windows, this might be called 32-Bit ODBC or simply ODBC.

The Data Source Administrator window appears. Figure 22.1 shows how this might look, although on your system the actual data sources shown might be different.

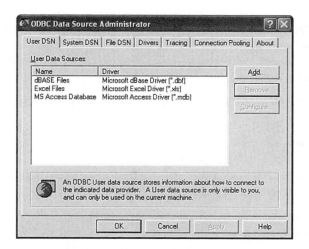

FIGURE 22.1 The ODBC Data Source Administrator.

Press the Add button to create a new data source. You will see a list of the data source drivers that are available on your system, similar to Figure 22.2.

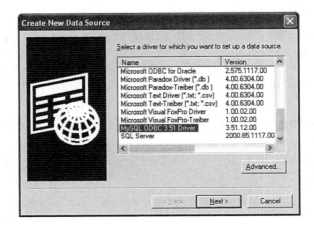

FIGURE 22.2   Data source driver selection.

Scroll down and select MySQL ODBC 3.51 Driver from the list; then press the Finish button. A new window opens containing the Connector/ODBC configuration. Here you should enter the connection details for your data source and give it an identifier.

Figure 22.3 shows the first tab of the Connector/ODBC configuration being completed.

Enter a new, unique name for this data source in the Data Source Name field. This will be used to identify your data source when you connect using ODBC. Description is an optional field where you can enter more information about this connection.

The Server value can be an IP address or the hostname of the MySQL server you want to connect to. Enter User and Password values that correspond to a valid user account on that MySQL server when connecting from the current host.

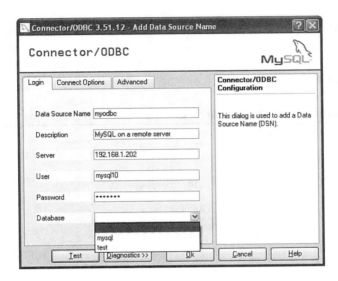

FIGURE 22.3   Connector/ODBC configuration.

Press the Test button to verify that your connection parameters are correct; if there are problems, use the Diagnostics button to view the error messages. When you have a successful connection, the Database menu will be populated with all the database names that the connected user can access. You can then select the database you want to use for this data source.

 Connection Port   If you need to set the TCP/IP port to a value other than the default (3306), this option is in the Connect Options tab in the Connector/ODBC configuration.

Press the OK button to save the new data source; you are returned to the Data Source Administrator window. You can adjust the connection parameters from here by selecting the data source name and pressing the Configure button.

Creating a Data Source on UNIX/Linux

On UNIX/Linux systems, data sources are defined in the `odbc.ini` file. The example in Listing 22.1 configures a DSN using the same parameters shown in Figure 22.3.

LISTING 22.1   Data Source Configuration in `odbc.ini`

```
[ODBC Data Sources]
myodbc      = MySQL on a remote server

[myodbc]
Driver      = /usr/local/lib/libmyodbc.so
Description = MySQL on a remote server
SERVER      = 192.168.1.202
PORT        =
USER        = mysql10
Password    = abc1234
Database    = mysql10
OPTION      = 3
SOCKET      =
```

You can specify multiple DSNs in this one file, giving each an entry in the [ODBC Data Sources] section and then giving the configuration specified using the DSN as a section heading in brackets. In this example, [myodbc] indicates the start of the connection parameters for that DSN.

An Example Connection from Excel

Now let's look at a very simple example of how to use a MySQL data source in an application that can fetch data using ODBC. Microsoft Excel can be configured to read table data from an external data source; using Connector/ODBC, the data can be fetched from a MySQL database table.

In the Data menu, select Get External Data and then New Database Query, as shown in Figure 22.4.

The Choose Data Source window appears and contains the DSNs available on your system. Select a MySQL data source—in the examples shown, the DSN is named myodbc and connects to a database named mysql10 that contains the sample tables used in this book (see Figure 22.5). Then press the OK button.

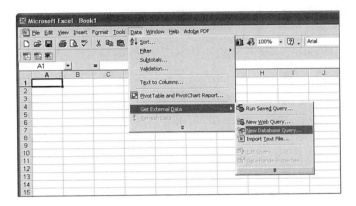

FIGURE 22.4   Connecting to an external data source in Excel.

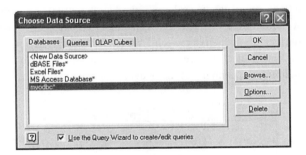

FIGURE 22.5   Selecting a Data source.

Next you will see the Query Wizard. This enables you to select the columns to pull through into your spreadsheet. As a simple example, simply select all the columns from the products table by selecting products and pressing the > button. The result is shown in Figure 22.6.

The remaining steps of the wizard can be used to generate more complex queries based on your MySQL data. You can select a filter condition and specify ordering, if desired. Behind the scenes, the Query Wizard is building an SQL query that is about to be passed to MySQL to fetch the corresponding data.

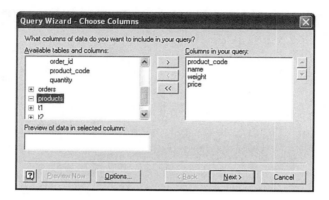

FIGURE 22.6   Selecting columns in the Query Wizard.

After the final step of the wizard, press the Finish button. You are asked to select a location in the spreadsheet for the data to be inserted—just select the default location, which is the top-left cell, assuming that you started with a blank worksheet. Figure 22.7 shows the result: an Excel spreadsheet containing the contents of the products table.

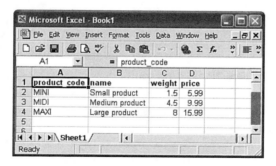

FIGURE 22.7   Excel spreadsheet after fetching data from MySQL.

Summary

In this lesson, you learned how to communicate with MySQL from a client program using ODBC. In the next lesson, you will learn about the native C API that enables you to interface with a database from your own programs.

LESSON 23

Using MySQL with C

In this lesson, you learn how to use the C API to develop your own applications.

The C Language API

The C Language API is the native programming interface for MySQL. In fact, virtually all the other APIs that are available use the C API. For example, the PHP interface, which you will learn about in Lesson 24, "Using MySQL with PHP," is written in C using this API. It contains many functions that map directly to a corresponding function in the underlying C library.

Client Programs The client utilities shipped with MySQL, such as `mysql` and `mysqladmin`, are all written using the C API. You can examine the source code for these if you want to see how they work.

Using the C API

The client library `libmysqlclient.so` contains the functions used to communicate with MySQL from a C program, and it is installed automatically if you compile MySQL from source. Your program must be linked using this library at compile time. Using the GCC compiler, use the following command to compile `myprog.c`:

```
$ gcc -o myprog myprog.c -lmysqlclient
```

Your programs must include the header file mysql.h, which is also installed automatically when building from source. It installs to a sub-directory off your include path—usually /usr/include/mysql/mysql.h—so your program must contain this statement at the beginning.

```
#include <mysql/mysql.h>
```

Binary Installation   When installing MySQL from a binary package or RPM, the distribution is split into separate components for the server, the client, and development. The packages containing the shared libraries and header files have names that begin with MySQL-shared- and then contain the version number and platform name.

For example, the current version of the RPM package for Red Hat Enterprise is named MySQL-devel-standard-5.0.18-0.rhel3.i386.rpm.

Finding the Compiler Options

The mysql_config utility shipped with MySQL enables you to find the correct compiler options to use when compiling a client program. Three possible switches can be passed to this utility to return the compiler flags, including the path and library options, as shown in the following examples. The responses shown might differ on your system.

```
$ mysql_config --cflags
-I/usr/include/mysql -mcpu=i486 -fno-strength-reduce

$ mysql_config --include
-I/usr/include/mysql

$ mysql_config --libs
-L/usr/lib/mysql -lmysqlclient -lz -lcrypt -lnsl -lm -lc
➥-lnss_files
   -lnss_dns -lresolv -lc -lnss_files -lnss_dns -lresolv
```

A failsafe way to pass all the correct compiler options to GCC is to use a shell escape, like this:

```
$ gcc -o myprog myprog.c 'mysql_config --cflags --include --libs'
```

Connecting to MySQL

The first MySQL API function you need to learn is how to connect to a MySQL database. This is actually done in two stages.

Firstly, you must initialize a new instance of a data structure that will become your connection reference for all future function calls using that database. The object must be declared as type MYSQL—note the unusual capitalization here—and you initialize it for use by the API by passing it to the mysql_init() function.

Next, you call the mysql_real_connect() function to initiate a connection to a MySQL database. Look at the example in Listing 23.1 first; we'll look at each value that can be passed as an argument in turn.

LISTING 23.1   Establishes a Connection to a MySQL Server

```
#include <stdio.h>
#include <mysql/mysql.h>

main() {

MYSQL mysql;

mysql_init(&mysql);
if (!mysql_real_connect(&mysql, "localhost",
                  "username", "password", "mysql10",
                  0, NULL, 0))
{
  fprintf(stderr, "Unable to connect to MySQL server\n");
}

}
```

Of course, this program does not really do anything beyond establishing a connection to the database and giving an error if the connection failed. For now, let this just serve as an example of how to create a database connection using the C API.

The return value from `mysql_real_connect()` is a MYSQL type object—in fact, the same value as the first argument—if the connection is successful, or NULL if it failed for any reason. We examine some more detailed error-reporting functions later in this chapter.

The `mysql_real_connect()` function takes eight arguments, with the function prototype shown here:

```
mysql_real_connect(&mysql, "host", "user", "password",
"dbname",
                port, unix_socket, client_flag);
```

These are the arguments:

1. `mysql`—The MYSQL type object that you initialized previously with `mysql_init()`.

2. `host`—The hostname of the MySQL server. This can be an IP address, domain name or hostname, or `localhost` for servers running on the same host as the client program.

3. `user`—The username for database authentication.

4. `passwd`—The password that corresponds to the username passed in argument 3.

5. `dbname`—The database name to connect to.

6. `port`—The port number for TCP/IP connections. For localhost connections or to use the default port, use `0` here.

7. `unix_socket`—The name of the socket or named pipe for local connections. For TCP/IP connections or to use the default socket, use NULL here.

8. `client_flag`—This argument can be used to enable certain features of the client library that are not covered in this book. Use `0` here unless you have a specific need.

Executing a Query

After you have established a connection to a MySQL server, you can issue a query to the database using the `mysql_query()` function. The first argument to this function is a connection reference. The second should be a null-terminated string that contains a single SQL query.

If the query you want to execute contains binary data, use `mysql_real_query()` instead. This function takes three arguments, with the third being the length of the query string. Using this function, any instances of the \0 character in your data are not treated as the null terminator in the string.

 Terminating Queries   The terminating semicolon is not required when you pass a query to `mysql_query()` or `mysql_real_query()`, but if you include it, it will not cause an error.

The return value from `mysql_query()` or `mysql_real_query()` is NULL to indicate success. If MySQL encounters an error, the function returns one of the values shown in Table 23.1.

TABLE 23.1   Error Codes Returned by `mysql_query()` or `mysql_real_query()`

Value	Meaning
CR_COMMANDS_OUT_OF_SYNC	Commands were executed in an improper order.
CR_SERVER_GONE_ERROR	The MySQL server has gone away.
CR_SERVER_LOST	The connection to the server was lost during the query.
CR_UNKNOWN_ERROR	An unknown error occurred.

If the return value is not NULL, you can call the `mysql_errno()` and `mysql_error()` messages to display the MySQL error number and message text, respectively. They each take a single argument, which is the connection handle.

Using the Result of a Query

If the query you pass to mysql_query() or mysql_real_query() is a
SELECT statement, it returns data that you want to fetch into your program.
The API functions that work with fetched data require a result resource
argument, which is a MYSQL_RES type of object.

To create a result handle, call the mysql_use_result() function. It takes a
single argument—a database connection handle—and returns a result
object that corresponds to the most recently executed query on that connection.

The return value from mysql_use_result() is either NULL to indicate success or one of the error values from Table 23.1. When a result handle has
been successfully assigned, you can continue to execute other queries
using the same database connection.

The most powerful way to fetch data from a result handle is with the
mysql_fetch_row() function. The first time you call mysql_fetch_row(),
the first row from the data set is returned and each subsequent call returns
the next row until no data remains to be fetched.

The data is returned into a MYSQL_ROW type structure, which contains one
element for each column returned by the query. The elements are numbered from zero, in the order they appear in the SELECT statement.

For example, suppose that your program executes the query SELECT
code, price FROM products ORDER BY price and then uses
mysql_fetch_row() to return the first row into a structure named result.
The value contained in result[0] will be the code for the first product
returned—with this query, the least expensive product in the table—and
result[1] will hold its price value.

The mysql_num_fields() function tells you the number of columns the
query returns. Using this in a loop, you can fetch a value from each
column. The example in Listing 23.2 uses this technique, along with the
other functions you have learned so far in this chapter, to produce a complete query example using the C API.

Counting Rows Returned Similar to `mysql num fields()`, you can use `mysql_num_rows()` to find the total number of rows a query returns.

LISTING 23.2   Performing a Query and Displaying the Results

```c
#include <stdio.h>
#include <mysql/mysql.h>

main() {

MYSQL mysql;
MYSQL_RES *result;
MYSQL_ROW row;
int numrows, numcols, c;

mysql_init(&mysql);

/* Establish a database connection */

if (!mysql_real_connect(&mysql, "localhost",
                "username", "password", "mysql10",
                0, NULL, 0))
{
  fprintf(stderr, "Error connecting: Error %d: %s\n",
                mysql_errno(&mysql), mysql_error(&mysql));
}

/* Execute a query */

char query[] = "SELECT * FROM customers ORDER BY name";

if (mysql_query(&mysql, query))
{
  fprintf(stderr, "Error executing query: Error %d: %s\n",
                mysql_errno(&mysql), mysql_error(&mysql));
}

/* Assign the result handle */

result = mysql_use_result(&mysql);
```

```
if (!result)
{
  fprintf(stderr, "Error using result: Error %d: %s\n",
                      mysql_errno(&mysql), mysql_error(&mysql));
}


/* Find the number of columns in the result */

numcols = mysql_num_fields(result);

/* Loop through the result set to display it */

while (row = mysql_fetch_row(result)) {
  for(c=0; c<numcols; c++) {
    printf("%s\t", row[c]);
  }
  printf("\n");
}

}
```

The output of this program is a tabulated list of columns, as follows:

```
MUSGRP  Musicians of America
PRESINC Presidents Incorporated
SCICORP Science Corporation
```

Using Other SQL Commands

You can issue other SQL commands than SELECT using mysql_query() or
mysql_real_query(), but they will not return a result. If you have the
appropriate permissions, you can issue UPDATE, INSERT, and DELETE statements on the database, and you could even perform a Data Definition
Language statement—the most common use for this is a CREATE
TEMPORARY TABLE statement in your application.

Using a Result   Attempting to call
mysql_use_result() after executing a SQL statement
that is not a SELECT is nonsense and produces an error.

The function `mysql_affected_rows()` can be used to determine the effect of an INSERT, UPDATE, or DELETE statement. It returns the number of rows affected by the SQL statement.

For INSERT and DELETE statements, this is a straight count of the number of rows added or removed by the operation. When the statement performed is an UPDATE, the return value from `mysql_affected_rows()` is the number of rows in which a value was changed from its previous value; this could be less than the total number of rows matched in the WHERE clause.

Tidying Up

To keep your program efficient, make sure you free up any resources that are no longer required.

Use `mysql_free_result()` to deallocate the resources associated with a result handle. After you have freed the result resource, you should not attempt to access it again in the program. This function takes a single argument, which is a MYSQL_RES type of object.

When you are done with the database connection altogether, use `mysql_close()` with a database handle as its argument to close the connection and free up the resource.

Summary

In this lesson, you learned how to communicate with a MySQL database from a program using the C API. In the next lesson, you will learn how to use the PHP API to create database-driven web pages.

LESSON 24

Using MySQL with PHP

In this lesson, you learn how to communicate with a MySQL database from a PHP script.

PHP actually has two different APIs for MySQL, both of which are covered in this chapter. The first, mysql, is the classic set of functions that are available in all versions of PHP.

The new interface is mysqli, which stands for MySQL Improved. It is available only in PHP version 5 and works only with MySQL version 4.1 and higher. The mysqli interface can be used through a set of functions or in an object-oriented manner, to fit the improved OO capabilities of PHP 5.

Using the mysql API

The classic mysql interface for PHP is a set of functions that map very closely to the C API functions you learned about in Lesson 23, "Using MySQL with C." To check whether this module is included in your PHP installation, create a simple script that simply contains the following line:

```php
<?php phpinfo();?>
```

View this script in a web browser and look for a section headed MySQL Support. If this section is not present, you will not be able to use the MySQL commands in PHP, and you will have to recompile PHP to include this module.

 Configuring PHP At compile time, MySQL support is enabled by using the --with-mysql configure switch. This option was enabled by default in PHP version 4 but is not in PHP 5.

Connecting to MySQL

Use the `mysql_connect()` function to establish a connection to a MySQL database. The first three arguments are the server hostname, username, and password for the connection. The following statement opens a new connection to a local MySQL server and assigns a connection handle named $conn:

```
$conn = mysql_connect("localhost", "user", "pass");
```

You must assign the connection handle resource returned by `mysql_connect()` so that you can use it later. Most MySQL API functions require this to be passed as an argument.

The `mysql_connect()` function prototype actually has five optional arguments:

1. `server`—The hostname of the MySQL server. This can be an IP address, domain name or hostname, or `localhost` where the MySQL server and web server are running on the same host.

2. `username`—The username for database authentication.

3. `password`—The password that corresponds to the username passed in argument 2.

4. `new_link`—Pass a nonzero value in this argument to cause a second call to `mysql_connect()` to create a separate database link. Otherwise, any existing connection will be reused.

5. `client_flags`—This argument can be used to enable certain features of the client library that are not covered in this book. Omit this argument unless you have a specific need.

Server Port There is no port argument in the `mysql_connect()` function. Instead, to change the TCP/IP port used, add a colon followed by the port number to the `server` argument—for example, `myserver.mydomain:1234`.

The return value from `mysql_connect()` is FALSE if the connection fails for any reason. You can then use the `mysql_errno()` and `mysql_error()` functions to return the MySQL error number and message text, respectively.

The argument to both error functions is a database connection handle, but the argument can be omitted if there is only one open connection in your script. The default behavior is to use the most recently opened connection.

The connection to the database server is made without selecting a database to work with. This must be done using a separate function, `mysql_select_db()`. The first argument is the name of the database to use. You can pass a connection handle as an optional second argument or omit this argument to use the most recently opened connection.

The following statement causes any queries executed using the `$conn` connection handle to use the `mysql10` database:

```
mysql_select_db("mysql10", $conn);
```

 Authentication Because selecting a database is done separately, the `mysql_connect()` function might succeed even if the database you intend to use is not available to the given user. You will receive an authentication error from `mysql_select_db()` if the user is not allowed to access the required database.

Listing 24.1 performs both steps, connecting to a MySQL server and selecting a database to use, with error checking along the way.

LISTING 24.1   Establishing a New Database Connection Using the Classic MySQL API

```php
<?php

$conn = mysql_connect("localhost", "user", "pass");
if (!$conn) {
  echo "Unable to connect to MySQL server <br>";
  echo "Error " . mysql_errno() . " - " . mysql_error();
```

```
  exit;
}

if (!mysql_select_db("mysql10")) {
  echo "Unable to select database <br>";
  echo "Error " . mysql_errno() . " - " . mysql_error();
  exit;
}

?>
```

Executing a Query

After you have established a connection to a MySQL server, you can execute a query using the `mysql_query()` function. This function takes two
arguments: a database connection handle and a string containing a single
SQL query. The terminating semicolon is not required. The following is
an example using a database resource named $conn:

```
$result = mysql_query($conn, "SELECT * FROM products");
```

The return value from `mysql_query()` is a result handle that you then use
to find information about the query and fetch records if the query was a
SELECT statement.

The result is FALSE if the query failed for any reason; you can then use
`mysql_errno()` and `mysql_error()` to find out more information.

Finding Information About a Query

If the query you executed was a SELECT statement, you can find how
many data rows it returned using the `mysql_num_rows()` function. It takes
a single argument—a query result handle returned by `mysql_query()`—
and returns the number of rows in the resulting data set. The following is
an example:

```
echo mysql_num_rows($result). " row(s) were returned";
```

The `mysql_num_fields()` function works in a similar manner and tells
you the number of columns in the data set.

If the query you executed was an UPDATE, INSERT, or DELETE statement, you can find out how many table rows were affected using the mysql_affected_rows() function. It also takes a result handle argument and returns the number of rows that were affected by the query.

 Affected Rows   If the query was an UPDATE statement, the value returned by mysql_affected_rows() will be the number of rows in which a value was changed from its previous value. This number might be less than the total number of rows matched by the WHERE clause.

Fetching Queried Data

The most powerful way to fetch data from a result handle is with the mysql_fetch_row() function. The first time you call mysql_fetch_row() on a result handle, the first row of data is returned and each subsequent call returns the next row until no data remains to be fetched.

The data is returned into an array that, by default, has both numeric and associative indexes. The elements are numbered from zero in the order they appear in the SELECT statement. They also have textual keys that correspond to the column name or alias from the query.

For example, suppose your script executes the query SELECT code, price FROM products ORDER BY price and then uses mysql_fetch_row() to return the first data row into $result. The value of $result[0] would be the code for the first product returned, and $result[1] would hold the corresponding price value. However, these values could also be accessed as $result["code"] and $result["price"].

Listing 24.2 puts everything together into a script that connects to MySQL, executes a query, and fetches and displays the resulting data.

LISTING 24.2   Performing a Query Using the Classic
MySQL API

```php
<?php

$conn = mysql_connect("localhost", "user", "pass");
if (!$conn) {
  echo "Unable to connect to MySQL server <br>";
  echo "Error " . mysql_errno() . " - " . mysql_error();
  exit;
}

if (!mysql_select_db("mysql10")) {
  echo "Unable to select database <br>";
  echo "Error " . mysql_errno() . " - " . mysql_error();
  exit;
}

$sql = "SELECT * FROM customers ORDER BY name";
$result = mysql_query($sql, $conn);
if (!$result) {
  echo "Unable to execute query <br>";
  echo "Error " . mysql_errno() . " - " . mysql_error();
  exit;
}

$numrows = mysql_num_rows($result);
$numcols = mysql_num_fields($result);

echo "<table border=1>\n";
while ($data = mysql_fetch_array($result)) {
  echo "<tr>";
  for ($i=0; $i<$numcols; $i++) {
    echo "<td>" . $data[$i] . "</td>\n";
  }
  echo "</tr>\n";
}
echo "</table>\n";

?>
```

The output from this script is in an HTML table format. Each time a new
record is fetched, the script outputs a <tr> tag and closes it with </tr> at
the end of the loop. Each individual data item is enclosed in <td> and

`</td>`. Running this script produces output similar to that shown in Figure 24.1.

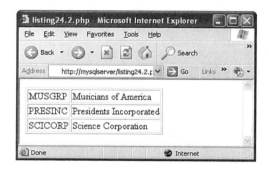

FIGURE 24.1   Output from sample query script.

Tidying Up

When your script has finished running, any associated resources are automatically deallocated. However you might want to do some housekeeping in your script to free up resources that you are done with.

The `mysql_free_result()` function destroys a result handle and deallocates its resources. You then cannot use that result handle with any of the mysql API functions.

The function `mysql_close()` takes a database handle argument. It disconnects from the MySQL server immediately and frees up the associated resources.

Using the mysqli API

To check whether your version of PHP includes mysqli support, run the `phpinfo()` command and look for a section headed `MySQLi Support`.

MySQLi Support   At compile time, MySQLi support is enabled by using the `--with-mysqli` configure switch. You might need to supply the path to the `mysql_config` utility, as in `--with-mysqi=/usr/bin/mysql_config`.

The MySQLi API can be used both procedurally and in an object-oriented manner. The procedural interface is very similar to the classic mysql API—for instance, it uses functions such as `mysqli_query()` and `mysqli_fetch_row()`. Therefore, in this section, you learn how to use MySQLi with objects.

Connecting to MySQL

The constructor function for a mysqli class object is used to initialize a MySQL connection. The following statement creates a new object with a connection to a database on the local host:

```
$conn = new mysqli("localhost", "user", "password", "mysql10");
```

The constructor function actually has six optional arguments:

1. `host`—The hostname of the MySQL server. This can be an IP address, domain name or hostname, or `localhost` where the MySQL server and web server are running on the same host.

2. `username`—The username for database authentication.

3. `passwd`—The password that corresponds to the username passed in argument 2.

4. `dbname`—The database name to connect to. Unlike in the mysql API, you do not need to make a separate function call to select the database.

5. `port`—The port number for TCP/IP connections. For `localhost` connections or to use the default port, omit this argument or pass `NULL`.

6. socket—The name of the socket or named pipe for local connections. For TCP/IP connections or to use the default socket, omit this argument or pass NULL.

If the connection fails, call the mysqli_connect_errno() and mysqli_connect_error() functions to find the MySQL error number and message text, respectively. Because the constructor function failed, you cannot call these functions as methods on a mysqli object.

Listing 24.3 creates a new mysqli database connection with error trapping.

LISTING 24.3   Establishing a New Database Connection Using the MySQLi API

```
<?php

$conn = new mysqli("localhost", "user", "pass", "mysql10");
if (mysqli_connect_errno()) {
  echo "Unable to connect to MySQL server <br>";
  echo "Error " . mysqli_connect_errno() . " - " .
➡mysqli_connect_error();
  exit;
}

?>
```

Executing a Query

When you have a mysqli object that is connected to a MySQL server, you can execute a query using the query() method. Its argument is a string that contains a single SQL query; the terminating semicolon is not required. The following statement is an example:

```
$result = $conn->query("SELECT * FROM customers");
```

If the query is successful, a result object is returned that then is used to find information about the query and to retrieve data rows if the query was a SELECT statement.

Otherwise, the return value is FALSE. You can check the errno and error properties on the connection object to find the MySQL error number and message text, respectively.

Object Properties Some pieces of information that are retrieved using functions in the classic mysql API or when using MySQLi procedurally become object properties instead of methods when you use MySQLi with objects.

For example, the function `mysqli_error()` becomes a property of a database connection object, `$conn->error`—note that there are no parentheses here.

Finding Information About a Query

If the query you executed was a SELECT statement, you can find how many data rows it returned by checking the `num_rows` property on the result object. It takes a single argument—a query result handle returned by `mysql_query()`—and returns the number of rows in the resulting data set. The following statement is an example:

```
echo $result->num_rows . " row(s) were returned";
```

The `field_count` property similarly contains the number of columns in the data set. The `affected_rows` property contains the number of rows affected by an UPDATE, INSERT, or DELETE statement.

Fetching Queried Data

The most powerful way to fetch data from a result handle is with the `fetch_object()` or `fetch_row()` methods. The first time you call `$result->fetch_object()`, the first row of data is returned. Each subsequent call returns the next row until no data remains to be fetched.

The data is returned into an object that contains a property for each column in the data set. The property's name is the same as the selected column name or alias in the query.

For example, suppose that your script executes the query SELECT code, price FROM products ORDER BY price and then uses `fetch_object()`

to return the first data row into $data. The value of $data->code would be the code for the first product returned—with this query, the least expensive product in the table—and $data->price would hold the corresponding price value.

The fetch_row() method works in the same way, except that it creates an array structure rather than an object, with each element indexed both numerically and associatively. Using the same example query, $data[0] and $data["code"] would both contain the product code.

Listing 24.4 puts everything together into a script that connects to MySQL, executes a query, and fetches and displays the resulting data.

LISTING 24.4   Performing a Query Using the MySQLi API

```php
<?php

$conn = new mysqli("localhost", "user", "pass", "mysql10");
if (mysqli_connect_errno()) {
  echo "Unable to connect to MySQL server <br>";
  echo "Error " . mysqli_connect_errno() . " - " .
➡mysqli_connect_error();
  exit;
}

$sql = "SELECT * FROM customers ORDER BY name";
$result = $conn->query($sql);

if (!$result) {
  echo "Unable to execute query <br>";
  echo "Error " . $result->errno . " - " . $result->error;
  exit;
}

echo "<table border=1>\n";
while ($data = $result->fetch_row()) {
  echo "<tr>";
  for ($i=0; $i<$result->field_count; $i++) {
    echo "<td>" . $data[$i] . "</td>\n";
  }
  echo "</tr>\n";
}
echo "</table>\n";

?>
```

This script uses the `fetch_row()` method to retrieve data because the output is generated in a loop. In many cases, you will know the column names for the data you are working with, and the `fetch_object()` method might be more convenient.

 MySQL vs. MySQLi   If you are familiar with another PHP database API, you will be familiar with the way the classic MySQL interface works. To see how the object-oriented MySQLi API compares, run through Listing 24.2 and Listing 24.4 step by step—they give exactly the same result.

Tidying Up

To deallocate a resource object, call the `$result->free()` method. Doing so destroys the object, so you no longer can call its methods or view its properties.

To disconnect from the database, call `$conn->close()`. The database connection is closed immediately and the connection object is destroyed.

Summary

In this lesson, you learned how to communicate with a MySQL server from a PHP script using both the available APIs. In the next lesson, you will learn how to use the Perl Database Interface with PHP.

LESSON 25
Using MySQL with Perl

In this lesson, you learn how to communicate with a MySQL database from a Perl script.

The Perl DBI

MySQL connectivity from Perl is handled in the same way that you can communicate with many other types of database: using the Perl Database Interface, or DBI.

If you have already used DBI with another database, you already know the essentials and will find it very easy to interface with MySQL.

DBI is independent of the database back ends and uses a specific database driver module, known as DBD, to interface with each DBMS.

If you do not already have DBI installed, use cpan to download and install it, as follows. You should either run this command as the root user on your system or have your system administrator run it for you.

```
# cpan
cpan> install DBI
```

The installation process produces a lot of output as it downloads and installs DBI and any other modules that it is dependent upon.

CPAN   The Comprehensive Perl Archive Network (CPAN) is a large collection of Perl software and documentation. The cpan utility is used to automatically download and install packages from this resource.

You also need to install a database driver for MySQL, which is called `DBD::mysql`. Enter this command at the `cpan>` prompt:

```
cpan> install DBD::mysql
```

On Windows systems using the ActivePerl distribution, use the `ppm.bat` script to install Perl modules, as follows:

```
C:\perl\bin> ppm.bat
ppm> install DBI
...
ppm> install dbd::mysql
```

Using the MySQL DBD

Any Perl script that uses DBI with the MySQL DBD module should begin with the following line:

```
use Mysql;
```

 Mysql Note the unusual capitalization of `Mysql` that is used in the Perl API. The name of this extension is case sensitive.

Connecting to MySQL

You establish a connection to a MySQL database by calling the `connect()` method on the master `Mysql` object. The following statement opens a new connection to the database `mysql10` on a local MySQL server and assigns a database handle named `$dbh`.

```
$dbh = Mysql->connect("localhost", "mysql10", "username",
➥"password");
```

`Mysql->connect()` should have exactly four arguments:

- `host`—The hostname of the MySQL server. This can be an IP address, domain name, or hostname. Use `undef` when the database server is `localhost`.

- dbname—The database name to connect to.

- user—The username for database authentication.

- password—The password corresponding to the username passed in argument 3.

The return value when a successful connection has been made is a database handle resource. If an error arises when connecting to the database, the properties errno and errstr on the master Mysql object will contain the MySQL error number of message text, respectively.

You can use a statement such as the following to perform a database connection with error trapping:

```
$dbh = Mysql->connect("localhost", "mysql10", "username",
➥"password")
    or die ("Error " . Mysql->errno . " - " . Mysql->errstr);
```

Executing a Query

When you have a database handle resource that is connected to a MySQL server, you can execute a query using the query() method on the database handle. Its argument should be a single SQL statement; the terminating semicolon is not required. The following statement is an example:

```
$sth = $dbh->query("SELECT * FROM customers");
```

The return value is a statement handle, which was assigned to $sth in this example. The statement handle is used to find information about the query and to retrieve data rows.

If an error occurs while executing the query, you can access the errno and errstr properties on the database handle object to retrieve the MySQL error number and message text, respectively.

You can use the following statement to execute a query and display the associated error message if there is a problem:

```
$sth = $dbh->query("SELECT * FROM products")
    or die("Error " . $dbh->errno . " - " . $dbh->errstr);
```

Finding Information About a Query

If the query you executed was a SELECT statement, you can find how many data rows it returned by checking the num_rows property on the statement handle. The following statement is an example:

```
print $sth->num_rows . " rows(s) were returned";
```

The num_fields property similarly contains the number of columns in the data set. The affected_rows property contains the number of rows affected by an UPDATE, INSERT, or DELETE statement.

Fetching Queried Data

When the fetchrow method is called on a statement handle, a row of data from the result of the query is returned into an array structure. No arguments are required.

The first time you call fetchrow(), the first row from the data set is returned; subsequent calls return the next row until there is no data left to be fetched.

The array elements are numbered from zero in the order they appear in the SELECT statement. For example, suppose that your script executes the query SELECT code, price FROM products ORDER BY price and then uses $sth->fetchrow to return a row of data into @data. The value in $data[0] will be the code for the first product returned, and $data[1] will be its price.

To reference data by its column name or alias, use the fetchrow_hash method. Using the previous example query and fetchrow_hash, you would be able to reference the values selected as $data->{code} and $data->{price}.

Listing 25.1 puts everything together into a script that connects to MySQL, executes a query, and fetches and displays the resulting data.

LISTING 25.1   Performing a Query Using the Perl DBI

```perl
#!/usr/bin/perl

use Mysql;

$dbh = Mysql->connect("localhost", "mysql10", "user", "pass")
  or die ("Error " . Mysql->errno . " - " . Mysql->errstr);

$sql = "SELECT * FROM customers ORDER BY name";
$sth = $dbh->query($sql)
  or die("Error " . $dbh->errno . " - " . $dbh->errstr);

while (@row = $sth->fetchrow) {
  for($i=0; $i<$sth->numfields; $i++) {
    print $row[$i] . "\t";
  }
  print "\n";
}
```

Running this script produces the output shown here: the contents of the customers table in tabulated format.

```
$ perl listing25.1.pl
MUSGRP  Musicians of America
PRESINC Presidents Incorporated
SCICORP Science Corporation
```

Tidying Up

Database connections opened in your script are automatically closed and resources are deallocated when the script ends. There is no specific function to explicitly disconnect from a database in the Perl DBI.

However, to free up any resources allocated in a running script, you can simply use undef to free the handle.

Summary

In this lesson, you learned how to use the Perl DBI with the MySQL DBD to communicate with a MySQL database from a Perl script. The last section of this book contains a number of appendixes for your reference.

APPENDIX A

Installing MySQL

This appendix shows you how to obtain and install MySQL if you do not already have it available to you.

Obtaining MySQL

The main downloads page for MySQL is http://dev.mysql.com/downloads/. This page tells you the latest major release version and provides a link to the next step of the download.

At the time of this writing, this page shows that the recommended current release is MySQL 5.0, with alpha releases of MySQL 5.1 also available. If you click through to download MySQL 5.0, you are taken to http://dev.mysql.com/downloads/mysql/5.0.html.

This page lists the MySQL downloads by platform, with a link to download each. The latest version number and the file size are displayed alongside each package.

The following sections explain which packages you require for each type of installation.

Linux/UNIX Installation

Follow these steps to install MySQL on a Linux/UNIX server. You must be logged in as the root user to install MySQL.

RPM Installation for Linux

If you are using a Linux system that supports RPM packages, such as Red Hat, SUSE, or Fedora, this is the easiest installation method to use. You simply download the appropriate packages and install them using the rpm utility.

The RPM distribution is split into the following packages. The filename prefix for each package is shown in parentheses.

- **Server** (MySQL-server)—The MySQL database server. You must install this package.

- **Client programs** (MySQL-client)—Contains the client programs for communicating with a MySQL server, including mysql and mysqladmin.

- **Libraries and header files** (MySQL-devel)—Development libraries and header files required for creating statically linked programs with the C API.

- **Dynamic client libraries** (MySQL-shared)—Shared libraries required for creating and running dynamically linked client programs.

- **Benchmark/test suites** (MySQL-bench)—A series of programs used to test the performance of a MySQL server.

The full filename of a package consists of the prefix shown in this list, the MySQL version number, and the platform it is compiled for.

For example, the latest version of the MySQL Server package for an Intel-based Linux system is installed from an RPM package named MySQL-server-5.0.18-0.i386.rpm.

Use the rpm command with the -i switch to install the RPM packages. If you have downloaded several packages, you can install them together by using the following command:

```
$ rpm -i MySQL*.rpm
```

 RPM Versions   Specific sets of RPM packages exist for Red Hat Enterprise Linux and SUSE Enterprise Linux. If you use one of these enterprise platforms, you must obtain the correct RPM versions.

RPM installation creates a service for MySQL. You can start the MySQL server by issuing the following command:

```
# /sbin/service mysql start
```

Binary Installation

If you are unable to use RPM, you will still likely find a precompiled binary version of MySQL available for your system.

 Binary Distribution   The precompiled binary distributions and RPM packages are highly optimized for a particular platform. You will usually achieve better performance from MySQL using the correct binary distribution than from a MySQL server you compiled from source.

The binary distribution of MySQL is a single compressed archive that contains the server, client programs, and development libraries. It is downloadable in a `.tar.gz` file—archived using `tar` and compressed using `gzip`. Three versions of each binary distribution exist: Standard, Max, and Debug.

- The Standard binaries are fine for most users—this is an optimized MySQL server with all the common features enabled at compile time.

- The Max binaries include additional features that are new or are not yet considered fully stable. You should consider using the Max distribution only if you have a specific need for it.

- The Debug binaries have additional debugging information compiled and are not suitable for general use. You should not use this distribution.

The binary download filename consists of `mysql-standard` (or `mysql-max`, for Max) followed by the version number and the platform. For example, if you are installing MySQL on an Intel-based OpenBSD system, the package you require will be named mysql-standard-5.0.16-openbsd3.7-i386.

After downloading the appropriate file, extract it using the following command. Use the cd command to navigate to the location where you want to install the files first: /usr/mysql and /usr/local/mysql are typical locations.

```
$ tar zxvf mysql-standard-5.0.16-openbsd3.7-i.386.tar.gz
```

Paths A binary installation does not automatically install its files to a location in your path. You will probably want to add /usr/mysql/bin or /usr/local/mysql/bin to your path for convenience.

To start the MySQL server, run the mysqld_safe program, which will have been installed to the bin directory. You should run this program in the background as follows:

```
# /usr/local/mysql/bin/mysqld_safe &
```

Installing from Source

MySQL is open source, so you are free to download the complete source code, if you want. This section deals with installing MySQL from source code.

The source code downloads appear at the very bottom of the downloads page. They are available as a .tar.gz file; the filename simply contains the version number.

Begin by extracting the latest version of the MySQL source to a suitable location, such as /usr/local/src.

```
# tar zxvf mysql-5.0.18.tar.gz
```

Next, run the configure program to allow the MySQL installation process to gather information about your system.

Compile-Time Configuration You can provide additional compile-time options here using switches to the configure program. For a list of the available switches and their default values, run `configure --help`.

```
# ./configure
```

The configure program generates a `Makefile`, so now you can run the make command to compile the MySQL server and client programs and the development libraries.

```
# make
```

Compiling MySQL might take some time, but when it is complete, you can install the various components to their correct locations by issuing a `make install` command.

Install Locations The default locations for a source installation are under `/usr/local` (`/usr/local/bin` for programs, `/usr/local/include` and `/usr/local/lib` for development files). Use the `--prefix` compile-time switch to specify a different location.

Windows Installation

Two different Windows installer programs are available for MySQL: the full distribution and a version called Windows Essentials that includes only the most popular features; Windows Essentials is about half the size of the full package. The Windows Essentials distribution, covered here, is suitable for most users.

First, download the latest version of the installer. The filename of the latest version at the time of this writing is `mysql-essetials-5.0.18-win32.msi`. Save this file to your desktop.

Double-click the installer icon to initiate the Setup Wizard. Click the Next button to advance to a screen like the one shown in Figure A.1.

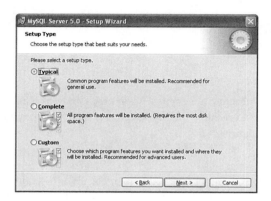

FIGURE A.1   The MySQL Setup Wizard.

Unless you have a specific reason to customize the installation, the default selection of Typical is fine. Click Next to continue.

The next screen confirms the location to which MySQL will be installed. Click the Install button to begin installation. It might take a few minutes for the MySQL installer to copy files.

The next window asks you to sign up for a MySQL.com account if you do not already have one. If you already have an account, enter your email address and password in the boxes. You can select Skip Sign-Up to skip this step, if you want. Click Next to continue.

Installation is now complete. You will see a window like the one shown in Figure A.2.

Click the Finish button to begin configuring the MySQL Server and launch the Configuration Wizard. Click Next; you will see the configuration type selection shown in Figure A.3.

Unless you have a specific need to change the installation settings, you can choose the option that requires the fewest decisions. Select Standard Configuration and click Next.

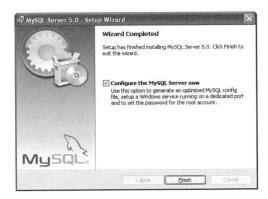

FIGURE A.2   After completing the MySQL Setup Wizard.

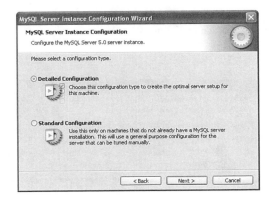

FIGURE A.3   MySQL Server Instance Configuration Wizard.

The window shown in Figure A.4 enables you to install MySQL as a
Windows service. This option is checked by default, and it's the easiest
way to get the MySQL server running.

If you check the box in the lower half of this window, the location of the
MySQL programs is added to your Windows PATH variable. This enables
you to invoke client programs from any system location without having to
enter their full path.

FIGURE A.4   Selecting whether to install MySQL as a Windows service.

The next window, shown in Figure A.5, requires you to set a new password for the root user.

FIGURE A.5   Security settings when configuring MySQL.

Remote Root Access Do not select the check box to enable root access from remote machines unless you are sure that you want to do this. Remember, you can always grant more privileges later. Even if you do want to allow remote superuser access, you should think about restricting it to certain IP addresses only. Refer to Lesson 18, "Managing User Access," for more information.

Enter a new password and confirm it by entering it a second time. Then click Next. The Configuration Wizard is ready to perform the configuration. Click the Execute button to continue.

MySQL installation is now complete. You will find a new program group called MySQL on your start menu; it contains a link to the configuration wizard in case you need to change any of the settings. There is also a link to the mysql command-line monitor.

To start and stop the MySQL service, select Control Panel, then Administrative Tools, and then Services. You can start, stop, pause, and restart the service from the Services manager.

APPENDIX B
Sample Table Scripts

As you follow each lesson in this book, you are strongly encouraged to try out each example on your own MySQL server.

The tables used by the examples throughout the book are created using the following SQL script. The script contains CREATE TABLE statements that define each table and some INSERT statements to populate the tables with their initial values.

> **Sample Database** You can download the SQL file printed here from the Sams Publishing website at http://www.samspublishing.com.

```
DROP TABLE IF EXISTS customers;

CREATE TABLE customers (
  customer_code VARCHAR(10)    NOT NULL,
  name          VARCHAR(40)    NOT NULL
);

INSERT INTO customers (customer_code, name)
VALUES ('PRESINC', 'Presidents Incorporated');

INSERT INTO customers (customer_code, name)
VALUES ('SCICORP', 'Science Corporation');

INSERT INTO customers (customer_code, name)
VALUES ('MUSGRP', 'Musicians of America');
```

```
DROP TABLE IF EXISTS customer_contacts;

CREATE TABLE customer_contacts (
    contact_id     INT             PRIMARY KEY AUTO_INCREMENT,
    customer_code  VARCHAR(10)     NOT NULL,
    first_name     VARCHAR(30)     NOT NULL,
    last_name      VARCHAR(30)     NOT NULL,
    email          TEXT,
    telephone      TEXT
);

INSERT INTO customer_contacts
    (customer_code, first_name, last_name, email)
VALUES ('PRESINC', 'Abraham', 'Lincoln',
➥'lincoln@presidentsinc.com');

INSERT INTO customer_contacts
    (customer_code, first_name, last_name, email)
VALUES ('PRESINC', 'Richard', 'Nixon',
➥'nixon@presidentsinc.com');

INSERT INTO customer_contacts
    (customer_code, first_name, last_name, email)
VALUES ('PRESINC', 'Franklin', 'Roosevelt',
➥'fdr@presidentsinc.com');

INSERT INTO customer_contacts
    (customer_code, first_name, last_name, email)
VALUES ('PRESINC', 'Theodore', 'Roosevelt',
➥'roosevelt@presidentsinc.com');

INSERT INTO customer_contacts
    (customer_code, first_name, last_name, email)
VALUES ('SCICORP', 'Albert', 'Einstein',
➥'einstein@sciencecorp.com');

INSERT INTO customer_contacts
    (customer_code, first_name, last_name, email)
VALUES ('SCICORP', 'Charles', 'Darwin',
➥'darwin@sciencecorp.com');

INSERT INTO customer_contacts
    (customer_code, first_name, last_name, email)
VALUES ('SCICORP', 'Marie', 'Curie', 'curie@sciencecorp.com');
```

```
INSERT INTO customer_contacts
  (customer_code, first_name, last_name, email)
VALUES ('SCICORP', 'Benjamin', 'Franklin',
►'franklin@sciencecorp.com');
INSERT INTO customer_contacts
  (customer_code, first_name, last_name, email)
VALUES ('MUSGRP', 'George', 'Gershwin', 'hawking@musgrp.com');

INSERT INTO customer_contacts
  (customer_code, first_name, last_name, email)
VALUES ('MUSGRP', 'Benjamin', 'Britten', 'britten@musgrp.com');

INSERT INTO customer_contacts
  (customer_code, first_name, last_name, email)
VALUES ('MUSGRP', 'John', 'Lennon', 'lennon@musgrp.com');


DROP TABLE IF EXISTS orders;

CREATE TABLE orders (
  order_id      INT             PRIMARY KEY AUTO_INCREMENT,
  customer_code VARCHAR(10)     NOT NULL,
  order_date    DATE            NOT NULL
);


DROP TABLE IF EXISTS order_lines;

CREATE TABLE order_lines (
  line_id       INT             PRIMARY KEY AUTO_INCREMENT,
  order_id      INT             NOT NULL,
  product_code  VARCHAR(10)     NOT NULL,
  quantity      TINYINT         NOT NULL
);


INSERT INTO orders (order_id, customer_code, order_date)
VALUES (1, 'PRESINC', '2006-01-23');

  INSERT INTO order_lines (order_id, product_code, quantity)
  VALUES (1, 'MINI', 4);

  INSERT INTO order_lines (order_id, product_code, quantity)
  VALUES (1, 'MAXI', 2);
```

```
INSERT INTO orders (order_id, customer_code, order_date)
VALUES (2, 'PRESINC', '2006-01-26');

  INSERT INTO order_lines (order_id, product_code, quantity)
  VALUES (2, 'MAXI', 12);


INSERT INTO orders (order_id, customer_code, order_date)
VALUES (3, 'SCICORP', '2006-01-23');

  INSERT INTO order_lines (order_id, product_code, quantity)
  VALUES (3, 'MINI', 16);


INSERT INTO orders (order_id, customer_code, order_date)
VALUES (4, 'SCICORP', '2006-02-02');

  INSERT INTO order_lines (order_id, product_code, quantity)
  VALUES (4, 'MINI', 16);

  INSERT INTO order_lines (order_id, product_code, quantity)
  VALUES (4, 'MAXI', 10);


INSERT INTO orders (order_id, customer_code, order_date)
VALUES (5, 'SCICORP', '2006-02-05');

  INSERT INTO order_lines (order_id, product_code, quantity)
  VALUES (5, 'MIDI', 10);

  INSERT INTO order_lines (order_id, product_code, quantity)
  VALUES (5, 'MAXI', 10);


INSERT INTO orders (order_id, customer_code, order_date)
VALUES (6, 'MUSGRP', '2006-02-01');

  INSERT INTO order_lines (order_id, product_code, quantity)
  VALUES (6, 'MAXI', 6);


INSERT INTO orders (order_id, customer_code, order_date)
VALUES (7, 'MUSGRP', '2006-02-02');
```

```
INSERT INTO order_lines (order_id, product_code, quantity)
VALUES (7, 'MAXI', 8);


DROP TABLE IF EXISTS t1;
CREATE TABLE t1 (
  id INT PRIMARY KEY,
  letter VARCHAR(1) NOT NULL
);

INSERT INTO t1 (id, letter) VALUES (1, 'A');
INSERT INTO t1 (id, letter) VALUES (2, 'B');
INSERT INTO t1 (id, letter) VALUES (3, 'C');

DROP TABLE IF EXISTS t2;
CREATE TABLE t2 (
  id INT PRIMARY KEY,
  letter VARCHAR(1) NOT NULL
);

INSERT INTO t2 (id, letter) VALUES (1, 'X');
INSERT INTO t2 (id, letter) VALUES (2, 'Y');
INSERT INTO t2 (id, letter) VALUES (3, 'Z');
```

Index

E

cross, 107, 114
equi, 108
inner, 108, 111-113
multiple tables, 109-113
natural, 116-117
outer, 117-118
self-joins, 115-116

keys. *See also* indexes
defining columns, 167-168
foreign, 166
constraints with InnoDB, 173-175
restrictions, 173
primary, 165
compound, 171
dropping, 170
viewing on table, 168-169

L

launching, command-line client (mysql), 10-11
LEFT JOIN keyword, SELECT statement, 118
LEFT JOIN operators, 124
LEFT OUTER JOIN keyword, SELECT statement, 118
lengths, data types, 162
libmysqlclient.so, 219-220
libraries
functions, 195
Linux/UNIX server installation, 246
LIKE operator, string comparisons, 65-66
LIMIT clause (SELECT statement)
limiting rows returned from queries, 46-47
skipping rows for queries, 47-48
limiting, rows returned from queries (LIMIT clause), 46-47
lines, terminator, 150
LINES STARTING BY command, 150

Linux
data source, 216
MySQL components, 7-8
MySQL installation
binary version, 247-248
RPM packages, 245-247
source code, 248-249
list of columns, retrieving (SELECT statement), 30
list of databases, retrieving (SELECT statement), 29
list of tables, retrieving (SELECT statement), 29
listings
Comma-Separated Data File with Column Headings, 150
Data Source Configuration in odbc.ini, 216
Error Codes Returned by mysql_query( ) or mysql_real_query( ), 223
MySQL Server Connection, 221
New Database Connection Using MySQLi API, 236
New Database Connection Using the Classic MySQL API, 230-231
Performing a Query and Displaying the Results, 225-226
Performing Query Using Classic MySQL API, 233-234
Performing Query Using MySQLi API, 238-239
Performing Query Using the Perl DBI, 244
Sample Tab-Separated Data File, 149
LOAD DATA INFILE command, 149-151
localhost, MySQL communication, 178
LOCATE( ) function, string location and replacement, 71
LOCK TABLES privilege, 179
LOG( ) function, 57
logarithms, LOG( ) function, 57